A Time to Laugh

A Time to Laugh

by
Bob Phillips

Harvest House Publishers
Irvine, California 92714

A TIME TO LAUGH
© 1977 by Harvest House Publishers,
Irvine, CA 92714
Library of Congress Catalog Card Number 76-53067
ISBN 0-89081-056-7
Printed in the United States of America.

ABDOMEN

A bowl-shaped cavity containing the organs of indigestion.

ABET

A gambling term.

ABILITY

The wind and the waves are always on the side of the ablest navigators.   Edward Gibbon

•   •   •

Executive ability is deciding quickly and getting somebody else to do the work.

ABSENT-MINDED

Did you hear about the absent-minded professor who:

Returned from lunch and saw a sign on his door, "Back in 30 minutes," and sat down to wait for himself?

Slammed his wife and kissed the door?

Got up and struck a match to see if he had blown out the candle?

ACCIDENT

A place where absence of body is better than presence of mind.

•   •   •

If four out of five accidents happen at home — why do people live there?

ACCURACY

Even a stopped clock is right twice a day.

ACCUSE

He that accuses all...convicts only one.

•   •   •

He who accuses too many accuses himself.

ACE

Damon Runyon used to tell this story on how he got his first newspaper job. It happened in Denver. He sat in the outer office patiently waiting while an office boy carried his request to be seen by the busy editor.

In about ten minutes the boy came back and said, "He wants you to send in a card." Runyon had no card, but being resourceful, he reached into his pocket and pulled out a deck of cards. From the deck he carefully extracted an ace and said, "Give him this."

He got in and he got the job.

ACHES AND PAINS

I've got so many aches and pains that if a new one comes today, it will be at least two weeks before I can worry about it.

ACHIEVEMENT

I feel that the greatest reward for doing is the opportunity to do more.   Jonas Salk

•   •   •

If you want a place in the sun, you have to expect some blisters.

•   •   •

Achievement is helping a person find out what he needs, then helping him to find the best way to get it.

ACQUAINTANCE

Jay: I understand you have a speaking acquaintance with her.

Bufe: Merely a listening acquaintance.

ACTION

Think like a man of action and act like a man of thought.

•   •   •

What you do speaks so loud that I cannot hear what you say.

Ralph Waldo Emerson

• • •

Actions speak louder than words — but not so often.

ACTOR

One who plays when he works.

ACUPUNCTURE

Acupuncture is nothing new. Most married men have been getting needled for years.

• • •

Acupuncture makes you wonder: Was it penicillin that cured us or just the needle?

• • •

There must be something to acupuncture — you never see any sick porcupines.

ADAM

Adam was the first man to know the meaning of rib roast.

• •

The best check-writing machine was made from Adam's rib.

ADAPTABILITY

The weathercock on the church spire, though made of iron, would soon be broken by the storm-wind if it...did not understand the noble art of turning to every wind.

ADMIRATION

Courageous foe is more to be admired than cowardly friend.

• • •

Admiration is the daughter of ignorance.

• • •

Distance is a great promoter of admiration!

• • •

A fool always finds a greater fool to admire him.

• • •

The feeling of delight that another person resembles us.

• • •

Admiration begins where acquaintance ceases.

ADOLESCENCE

A fellow mentioned that his teenage son was developing a cauliflower ear. Not from boxing — but from using the phone.

• • •

Adolescence is that time of life when children start bringing up their parents.

• • •

Adolescence is that time in a boy's life when he notices that a girl notices he is noticing her.

ADVANTAGE

Every disadvantage has its advantage.

ADVENTURE

You can't cross the sea merely by standing and staring at the water. Don't let yourself indulge in vain wishes.

• • •

Intrigued by an ad for "An Adventure Cruise to Nowhere," a man signed up and paid his $500 in advance. He appeared at the wharf on the day of the sailing. Suddenly, a huge man grabbed him, forcibly dragged him below deck, shackled him to a bench and shoved a galley oar at him. For two long weeks the vacationist rowed, pulling in time to an incessant drumbeat, with another adventure-cruiser chained to the bench beside him.

Upon reaching the wharf again, the oarsmen were unshackled, and the cruise was over. At this moment, the first chap turned to his rowing mate and said, "I'm not informed as to the amenities involved in these adventure cruises. Should we tip the drummer?"

ADVERSITY

The brook would lose its song if we removed the rocks.

•   •

Gold is tried by fire, brave men by adversity.   Seneca

•   •   •

There's no sense in advertising your troubles — there's no market for them.

•   •   •

The darker the day, the more we must pray. The darker the days, the more we should praise.

•   •   •

You are a poor specimen if you can't stand the pressure of adversity.   Proverbs 24:10

ADVERTISING

Doing business without advertising is like winking at a girl in the dark. You know what you are doing, but nobody else does.

•   •   •

Samson had the right idea about advertising. He took two columns and brought down the house.

ADVICE

Advice is seldom welcome, and those who need it the most, like it the least.   Lord Chesterfield

•   •   •

We give advice by the bucket, but take it by the grain.
          William Alger

•   •   •

He that gives good advice, builds with one hand; he that gives good counsel and example, builds with both; but he that gives good admonition and bad example, builds with one hand and pulls down with the other.
          Francis Bacon

•   •   •

Write down the advice of him who loves you, though you like it not at present.

•   •   •

He who gives advice to a self-conceited man stands himself in need of counsel.
          La Rochefaucauld

•   •   •

He who can take advice is sometimes superior to him who can give it.

•   •   •

It's surprising how many persons unselfishly will neglect their own work in order to tell you how to run your affairs.

•   •   •

Though good advice lies deep within a counselor's heart, the wise man will draw it out. Proverbs 20:5

•   •   •

Better ask twice than lose your way once.

•   •   •

Young man, consult your father. He is often as old as you are, and sometimes knows as much.

•   •   •

Socrates was a Greek philosopher who went around giving good advice. They poisoned him.

•   •   •

We are never so generous as when giving advice.

• • •

Timely advice is as lovely as golden apples in a silver basket.
                              Proverbs 25:11

• • •

Is it possible to expect mankind to take advice when they will not so much as take warning?   Swift

• • •

He is bad that will not take advice, but he is a thousand times worse who takes every advice.

• • •

If you are looking for advice, stay away from fools. Proverbs 14:7

• • •

Everyone enjoys giving good advice, and how wonderful it is to be able to say the right thing at the right time!   Proverbs 15:23

• • •

Ability to give wise advice satisfies like a good meal!
                              Proverbs 18:20

• • •

Get all the advice you can and be wise the rest of your life.
                              Proverbs 19:20

• • •

The best way to succeed in this world is to act on the advice you give to others.

• • •

Perhaps one of the reasons why we get so much free advice is that it's easier than helping.

• • •

Never trust the advice of a man in difficulties.

• • •

A fool thinks he needs no advice, but a wise man listens to others.   Proverbs 12:15

• • •

People who offer good advice always offer it in the big economy size.

• • •

Advice is like snow; the softer it falls, the longer it dwells upon, and the deeper it sinks into the mind.   Coleridge

• • •

If you wish good advice, consult an old man.

• • •

Only a fool despises his father's advice; a wise son considers each suggestion.   Proverbs 15:5

• • •

There is an old story of an Eastern merchant who was about to send his eldest son forth into the world. "My son," said the merchant, "there are two precepts I would have you keep ever in mind. The first of these is, 'Always keep your word once you have given it.'"

"Yes, Father," said the son. "And the second?"

"Never give it."

AEROSOL

Man to man: "A few years ago, a mad scientist needed an atomic bomb to destroy the earth. Now, all he needs is an aerosol can."

AFFECTION

Caresses, expressions of one sort or another, are necessary to the life of the affections as leaves are to the life of a tree. If they are wholly restrained, love will die at the roots.

• • •

Above all else, guard your affections. For they influence everything else in your life.

Proverbs 4:23

AFFLICTION

Affliction, like the iron-smile, shapes as it smites.

• • •

Affliction is God's shepherd dog to drive us back to the fold.

• • •

The gem cannot be polished without friction, nor man perfected without trials.

• • •

As sure as God puts His children into the furnace of affliction He will be with them in it.

Charles Haddon Spurgeon

AFTER-DINNER SPEAKER

The guy who starts the bull rolling.

AGE

At 20 years of age the will reigns, at 30 the wit; at 40 the judgment.   Benjamin Franklin

• • •

Age does not depend upon years, but upon temperament and health. Some men are born old, and some never grow so.

• • •

The woman who tells her age is either too young to have anything to lose or too old to have anything to gain.

• • •

The older I grow the more I distrust the familiar doctrine that age brings wisdom.

• • •

Her age is her own business — and it looks like she's been in

business a long time.

• • •

At age 20, we don't care what the world thinks of us. At 30, we begin to worry what it thinks of us. At 50, we find it wasn't thinking of us at all.

• • •

The judge pounded his gavel for the court to come to order, then turned to the woman in the witness box.

"The witness will please state her age," he ordered, "after which she will be sworn in."

• • •

Never ask a woman her age; ask it of some other woman.

• • •

It's surprising how many persons our age are a lot older than we are.

AGNOSTIC

A person who says that he knows nothing about God and, when you agree with him, he becomes angry.

• • •

Agnostic is Latin for ignoramus.

AGGRAVATING

Think twice before you speak and you may say something even more aggravating.

AGREE

When two men in a business always agree, one of them is unnecessary. William Wrigley, Jr.

AGREEMENT

You may easily play a joke on a man who likes to argue — agree with him.

• • •

There is no conversation more boring than the one where everybody agrees.

• • •

He that complies against his will is of his own opinion still.

Samuel Butler

AHEAD

A good thing to have.

AIM

In great attempts it is glorious even to fail.

AIR-CONDITIONED

Why is it a businessman will go from his air-conditioned house to his air-conditioned office in his air-conditioned car, then go to a health club and pay $50 an hour to sweat?

ALIMONY

Check Mate. Taking advantage of bank checks personally designed to express individuality, a California man had a set of checks imprinted with a photograph of himself kissing his new young wife — to be used exclusively to send alimony payments to his ex-wife.

ALLOWANCE

Son to father: "About my allowance, Pop. It's fallen below the national average for teenagers."

ALONE

A person who is alone isn't necessarily in good company.

AMBITION

Some folks can look so busy doin' nothin' that they seem indispensable.

• • •

You can't hold a man down without staying down with him.

Booker T. Washington

• • •

An itching sensation caused by inflammation of the wishbone.

• • •

If I shoot at the sun I may hit a star.   P.T. Barnum

AMERICA

A citizen of America will cross the ocean to fight for democracy, but won't cross the street to vote in a national election.

• • •

America is the country where you buy a lifetime supply of aspirin for one dollar and use it up in two weeks.   John Barrymore

AMIABILITY

An inexhaustible good nature is one of the most precious gifts of heaven, spreading itself like oil over the troubled sea of thought, and keeping the mind smooth and equable in the roughest weather.

Washington Irving

AMISS

Someone who is not married.

AMMONIA

Lisa: Don't you know the difference between ammonia and pneumonia?

Chris: Sure, one comes in bottles and the other in chests.

ANALYST

The analyst is not a joke: He finds you cracked, and leaves you broke.

ANGELS

God made man a little lower than the angels, and he has been getting a little lower ever since.

Will Rogers

• • •

All women are angels, but there are two sorts of angels.

ANGER

He is a fool who cannot be angry; but he is a wise man who will not.

● ● ●

Whenever you are angry, be assured that it is not only a present evil, but that you have increased a habit. Epictetus

● ● ●

Keep cool; anger is not an argument. Daniel Webster

● ● ●

Anger is as a stone cast into a wasp's nest.

● ● ●

The greatest remedy for anger is delay. Seneca

● ● ●

When a man is wrong and won't admit it, he always gets angry.

● ● ●

I was angry with my friend,
I told my wrath, my wrath did end.
I was angry with my foe.
I told it not, my wrath did grow.
William Blake

● ● ●

Anger blows out the lamp of the mind. Robert Green Ingersol

● ● ●

A little pot
Is soon hot.

ANNOY

A man is as big as the things that annoy him.

ANONYMOUS

The name of a joke book writer.

ANSWER

A soft answer turns away wrath, but harsh words cause quarrels.
Proverbs 15:1

ANT

None preaches better than the ant, and she says nothing. Franklin

ANTICIPATION

If pleasures are greatest in anticipation, just remember that this is also true of trouble.

ANTIQUE

Clerk: This is an ancient Roman candlestick.
Buyer: Are you sure you are not trying to fool me. Is it really that old?
Clerk: Old, when they dug it up, it had written on it 300 B.C.

ANXIETY

Anxiety is the poison of human life.

APATHY

The No. 1 problem in our country is apathy...But who cares!

APOSTLE PAUL

Question: When was the Apostle Paul a baker?
Answer: When he went to Philippi.

APPEARANCE

You are only what you are when no one is looking.

● ● ●

Abstain from all appearance of evil. I Thessalonians 5:22, KJV

● ● ●

Susie: Which would you desire most in your husband, brains, wealth or appearance?
Rosie: Appearance...and the sooner the better.

APPETITE

A well-governed appetite is a great part of liberty.   Seneca

●   ●   ●

Carry an appetite to God's house, and you will be fed.

APPLAUSE

Let's have a round of applause for the wonderful job the program committee did in not being able to obtain a speaker.

●   ●   ●

Robert Montgomery's advice concerning applause: "Enjoy it, but never quite believe it."

APPLE

Something that was stuck in Adam's throat.

●   ●   ●

Handsome apples are sometimes sour.

●   ●   ●

While visiting a friend who was in the hospital, I noticed several pretty nurses, each of whom was wearing a pin designed to look like an apple. I asked one nurse what the pin signified.

"Nothing," she said with a smile. "It's just to keep the doctors away."

APPRECIATION

First man
at bar: "My wife doesn't appreciate me. Does yours?"

Second man
at bar: "I would not know. I've never heard her mention your name.

●   ●   ●

The only place in some homes where appreciation can be found is in the dictionary.

●   ●   ●

"How can I ever show my appreciation?" gushed a woman to a famous lawyer, after he had solved her legal troubles.

"Madam," he replied, "ever since the Phoenicians invented money there's been only one answer to that question."

●   ●   ●

Appreciation is the memory of the heart.

APPOINTMENT

Not keeping an appointment is an act of clear dishonesty. You may as well borrow a person's money as his time.   Horace Mann

ARCHAEOLOGIST

A man whose career lies in ruins.

ARGUMENT

If you really want the last word in an argument, try saying, "I guess you're right."

●   ●   ●

I always get the better when I argue alone.

●   ●   ●

Something you do with a fool, but be sure he isn't similarly engaged.

●   ●   ●

He who establishes his argument by noise and command shows that his reason is weak.

●   ●   ●

Behind every argument is someone's ignorance.

●   ●   ●

A long dispute means both parties are wrong.

• • •

The only way to get the best of an argument is to avoid it.

Dale Carnegie

• • •

The good man wins his case by careful argument; the evil-minded only wants to fight.   Proverbs 13:2

• • •

There is no boxing match with only one person.

ARSENIC

"I want some arsenic for my mother-in-law."

"Have you a prescription?"

"No, but here's her picture."

ART

If my husband would ever meet a woman on the street who looked like the women in his paintings, he would fall over in a dead faint.

Mrs. Pablo Picasso

• • •

Art, like morality, consists in drawing the line somewhere.

Gilbert K. Chesterton

ARTIC CIRCLE

She's so cold she has artic circles under her eyes.

ASHAMED

Live in such a way that you would not be ashamed to sell your parrot to the town gossip.

Will Rogers

ASSASSINATION

Assassination: the extreme form of censorship.

George Bernard Shaw

ASTRONAUT

The astronaut was preparing for his moon launch and being interviewed by the press. "How do you feel?" asked one reporter.

"How would you feel if you were going to the moon in a vehicle with over 150,000 parts and you knew they were all supplied by the lowest bidder?"

ASTRONOMY

Astronomy is over your head.

ATHEISM

Nobody talks so constantly about God as those who insist that there is no God.

• • •

I am an atheist, thank God!

• • •

An atheist is one point beyond the devil.

• • •

Some are atheists only in fair weather.

• • •

By night an atheist half believes a god.

ATMOSPHERE

What is known as congestion in a subway is called atmosphere in a nightclub.

ATOM

The professor of a technical class was conducting an experiment with atoms. At the end, he commented: "Now observe that at the beginning of this experiment there were twenty-seven atoms. Now there are only twenty-six."

Then he asked, "What happened to that other atom, students?"

After several moments of tense silence, a low voice from the back of the room said, "Nobody leave this room."

ATP

Question: What is A T P?
Answer: It is what the Indians live in.

ATTEMPTED

Samuel Johnson wrote: "Nothing will ever be attempted if all possible objections must be first overcome."

ATTENTION

Hold the ear, and the head will follow.

ATTITUDE

As he thinketh in his heart, so is he.   Bible

•   •   •

A relaxed attitude lengthens a man's life; jealousy rots it away.
                    Proverbs 14:30

•   •   •

When we are flat on our backs there is no way to look but up.

•   •   •

Those who wish to sing always find a song.

AUCTION

Auction — A place where you are liable to get something for nodding.

AUCTIONEER

The auctioneer interrupted his chanting to announce that someone in the crowd had lost their billfold containing $1,000 and that he was offering a reward of $200 for its return.

A voice from the rear of the crowd piped up, "I'll bid $210."

AUTHOR

An author retains the singular distinction of being the only person who can remain a bore long after he is dead.

•   •   •

'Tis pleasant, sure, to see one's name in print;
A book's a book, although there's nothing in't.   Byron

AVERAGE

Not doing more than the average is what keeps the average down.

•   •   •

Average is the best of the worst and the worst of the best.

AVON LADY

Bob: What is blue and goes ding dong?
Ken: An Avon lady at the North Pole.

AX

People with an ax to grind often fly off the handle.

BABY

An alimentary canal with a loud voice at one end and no responsibility at the other.

•   •   •

Tommy: "Say, Mom, was our baby sent down from heaven?"
Mother: "Yes, son."
Tommy: "I guess they like to have things quiet up there, huh?"

BABY-SITTER

Someone you employ to watch your television set.

BACHELOR

A man who's been lucky at love.

•   •   •

Nancy: What excuse have you for not being married?
Rich: I was born that way.

•   •   •

Joan: "Hasn't Jack ever married?"

Jean: "No, I don't think he intends to, because he's studying for a bachelor's degree."

• • •

Bachelor: One who's footloose and fiancee free.

• • •

A bachelor is a man who prefers to go through life wanting something he doesn't have rather than having something he doesn't want.

BACHELOR GIRL

A girl who is still looking for a bachelor.

BAGDAD

What mother did when she met father.

BAIT

They had been married just two weeks and he was going through a batch of mail that had arrived.

"Honey," he said, "aren't these bills for clothes you bought before we were married?"

"Yes, darling," she replied. "You aren't upset about it are you?"

"Not really," he replied. "But don't you think it's a bit unfair to ask a fish to pay for the bait he was caught with?"

BAKERY

"You're the object of our confections."

BALANCED BUDGET

Question: What is a balanced budget?

Answer: When money in the bank and the days of month come out together.

BALD

It's like heaven; there is no dying or parting there.

• • •

Hair by hair the head grows bald.

• • •

The penalty of being a highbrow.

BALLET

A little boy who went to the ballet for the first time with his father watched the girls dance around on their toes for a while, and then asked, "Why don't they just get taller girls?"

BANANA

Dave: If something is yellow and looks like a banana and smells like a banana how do you know if it's really a banana?

Dick: Listen and see if it makes a noise like a banana.

BARBED

As the fat man said when he crawled through the barbed wire fence, "One more point and I'm through."

BARBER

A brilliant conversationalist, who occasionally shaves and cuts hair.

• • •

It is getting so a good barber can earn as much per word as an author.

BARGAIN

On a good bargain think twice.

• • •

Think twice over a great bargain, and then leave it.

• • •

"Utterly worthless!" says the buyer as he haggles over the price. But afterwards he brags about his bargain! Proverbs 20:14

• • •

Good bargains are pickpockets.

BARK
Barking dogs never bite...while barking.

BARTENDER
"Papa, what is the person called who brings you in contact with the spirit world?"

"A bartender, son."

BATH
Every man has the right to a Saturday night bath and many need to exercise their rights.

BAY
The dog may bay but still the moon stands steady as before.

BEANS
They serve a balanced diet in the Army. Every bean weighs the same.

BEAR
If you go hunting bear, you'll catch cold.

BEARD
"Once I had a beard like yours, and when I saw how terrible I looked, I got it cut off."

"I used to have a face like yours, too, and when I saw how terrible it made me look I grew a beard."

BEAUTY
There are no ugly women; there are only women who do not know how to look pretty.

Lisa: My fiance has been telling everybody that he is going to marry the most beautiful girl in the world.

Chris: Oh, what a shame! And after all the time you've been going with him.

• • •

Beauty is worse than wine; it intoxicates both the holder and the beholder.

• • •

Beauty is like a rainbow — full of promise but short-lived.

Josh Billings

• • •

To marry a woman for her beauty is like buying a house for its paint.

BED
As you make your bed, so you must lie on it.

BEFRIEND
When befriended, remember it; When you befriend — forget it.

BEHAVIOR
Behavior is a mirror in which everyone displays his image.

Johann Wolfgang von Goethe

• • •

Be nice to people on your way up because you'll meet them on your way down.

• • •

The reason the way of the transgressor is hard is because it's so crowded.

• • •

The man who wears his pants out before his shoes, makes contact in the wrong places.

•   •   •

Some folks don't have many faults, but they sure make the most of those they've got.

BEHIND
He who rides behind another does not travel when he pleases.

BELIEF
Strong beliefs win strong men, and then make them stronger.

•   •   •

Philosopher Bertrand Russell, asked if he was willing to die for his beliefs, replied: "Of course not. After all, I may be wrong."

•   •   •

One person with a belief is equal to a force of ninety-nine who have only interests.

BELL
"I just adore lying in my bed in the morning and ringing my bell for my maid."

"My goodness, I didn't know you had a maid."

"I don't, but I have a bell."

•   •   •

One day a stranger approached Mark Twain with a request for $500 for which he would sell half interest in his invention. Twain, "bit" several times before, refused flatly. But out of courtesy he asked the stranger his name. "Bell," the man replied, turning away, "Alexander Graham Bell."

BEST
"How can you treat me like that after I gave you the best years of my life?"

"Good grief...those were your best?"

BIBLE
Most people are bothered by those passages of Scripture they do not understand, but the passages that bother me are those I do understand.   Mark Twain

•   •   •

Be careful how you live; you may be the only Bible some person ever reads.

•   •   •

Thy word is a lamp unto my feet, and a light unto my path.
                    Psalms 119:105, KJV

•   •   •

The family Bible can be passed down from generation to generation because it gets so little wear.

•   •   •

Despise God's Word and find yourself in trouble. Obey it and succeed.   Proverbs 13:13

•   •   •

But the Word of the Lord endureth for ever. I Peter 1:25, KJV

•   •   •

The reason people are down on the Bible is that they're not up on the Bible.   William Ward Ayer

•   •   •

Sin will keep you from this book. This Book will keep you from sin.   Dwight L. Moody

•   •   •

Men do not reject the Bible because it contradicts itself but because it contradicts them.

BIGAMIST
Someone who makes the same mistake twice.

BIGOT
The mind of the bigot is like the pupil of the eye; the more light

you pour upon it, the more it will contract.   O.W. Holmes

• • •

Without a single exception, we have always found that the narrow-minded bigots are the ones who disagree with us.

BILLS

Woman to bill paying husband: "I slashed expenses last month — everything was charged on one credit card so that it will take only one postage stamp to pay our bills."

• • •

We never get anything but sad news out of those envelopes with a window in front.

BIRTH

If nature had arranged that husbands and wives should have children alternately, there would never be more than three in a family.

BIRTHDAY

Husband to wife: "How do you expect me to remember your birthday when you never look any older?"

BIRTHSTONE

Son: Dad, this magazine article says that my birthstone is the ruby. What is yours?

Father: The grindstone.

BLAME

He wrecked his car, he lost his job, and yet throughout his life, he took his troubles like a man — he blamed them on his wife!

• • •

To err is human; to blame it on the other guy is even more human.

• • •

You are not a failure until you blame someone else.

BLANK

Randy: "Did you fill in the blank yet?"

Andy: "What blank?"

Randy: "The one between your ears."

BLASTS

The number of blasts that come from auto horns in a traffic jam is equal to the sum of the squares at the wheels.

BLIND

None so blind as those that will not see.   Matthew Henry

BLINDNESS

Joe: He went blind from drinking coffee.

Moe: How did it happen?

Joe: He left his spoon in the cup.

BLIZZARD

A blizzard is the inside of a fowl.

BLOC

A minority group often led by someone called a bloc head.

BLOOD

The blood of the martyrs is the seed of the church.   Tertullian

BLOW

He who blows in the dust will hurt his own eyes.

BLUE JEANS

What people used to wear who worked.

BLUNDER

Mark Twain was once asked the difference between a mistake and a blunder. He explained it this way. "If you walk into a restaurant and walk out with someone's silk umbrella and leave your own cotton one, that is a mistake. But if you pick up someone's cotton umbrella and leave your own silk one, that's a blunder.''

BLUSH

Man is the only animal that blushes. Or needs to.   Mark Twain

•   •   •

A man took his daughter on a trip to New York and went to one of those plays that made the father blush a bit.

''I'm sorry, Dorothy, that I brought you here,'' he said. ''This is hardly a place for a girl of your age.''

''Oh, that's all right, Dad. It'll probably liven up a bit before too long.''

BOAST

Someone who opens his mouth and puts his feats in.

•   •   •

The man that talks much about himself will have a tired audience.

BOLDNESS

When you cannot make up your mind which of two evenly balanced courses of action you should take — choose the bolder.

BONE

Some people have a lot of it in their head.

•   •   •

The bone of contention is the jawbone.

•   •   •

I work my head to the bone.

BOOK

The man who does not read good books has no advantage over the man who can't read them.

Mark Twain

•   •   •

A bad book is the worst of thieves.

•   •   •

Martin Luther said once that ''The multitude of books is a great evil.''

•   •   •

For people who like that kind of a book — that is the kind of book they will like.

—Lincoln, on being asked for an opinion

•   •   •

Sign in the Atlanta Public Library: ''Books do not pause to deliver a message from their sponsors.''

•   •   •

Where is human nature so weak as in the bookstore?

H. W. Beecher

•   •   •

The love of books is an infectious sort of thing. Children catch it, they don't learn it.

BORE

A person who has flat feats.

•   •   •

A bore is a person who is me-deep in his conversation.

•   •   •

A bore is someone who persists in holding his own views after we have enlightened him with ours.

•   •   •

Mark Twain was once trapped by a bore who lectured to him about the hereafter: ''Do you realize that every time I exhale my breath, some poor soul leaves this world and passes on to the great beyond?''

''Really. Why don't you try chewing cloves?''

• • •

We often forgive those who bore us but we cannot forgive those whom we bore.   La Rochefoucauld

• • •

At a formal dinner the hostess, who was seated at the far end of the table from a very famous actress, wrote a note to the actress and had the butler deliver it.

The actress couldn't read without her glasses, so she asked the man at her left to read it to her. ''It says,'' he began, ''Dear, do me a favor and please don't neglect the man at your left. I know he's a bore, but talk to him.''

BORROWING

He who borrows sells his freedom.

• • •

Live within your income, even if you have to borrow money to do so.   Josh Billings

BOTTLENECK

The bottleneck is always at the top.

BOTTOM

It's a good idea to begin at the bottom in everything except in learning to swim.

BOSS

It's easy to tell who the boss is. He's the one who watches the clock during the coffee break.

BOY

Boys will be boys, and so will a lot of middle-aged men.

• • •

An appetite with a skin pulled over it.

• • •

One of the best things in the world to be is a boy; it requires no experience, but needs some practice to be a good one.

BOYFRIEND

A boyfriend is a fellow who lost his liberty in the pursuit of happiness.

BRAIN FOOD

Question: Is there any other brain food besides fish?

Answer: Yes, Noodle Soup.

BRAINS

Don: She's a bright girl...she has brains enough for two.

Art: Then she's just the girl for you.

• • •

''How long can a man live without brains?''

''I don't know. How old are you?''

BRAT

A child who acts like yours but belongs to a neighbor.

BRAVE

It is easy to be brave from a safe distance.   Aesop

BREAKDOWN

The big trouble with success is that the formula is the same as for a nervous breakdown.

BREVITY

Brevity is a fine thing in a speech.

BRIDEGROOM

The proof that a woman can take a joke.

BRIDLE

Better a bridle on the tongue than a lash upon the conscience.

BRIDLE PATH

Dora: "Why didn't you ride in the bridle path?"

Nora: "I thought that was only for newly married couples."

BRIEFLY

After-dinner speaking is the art of saying nothing briefly.

BRUSHING

One thing about getting old is that you can sing in the bathroom while brushing your teeth.

BUDGET

A group of figures that prove you shouldn't have gotten married in the first place.

• • •

Teacher: "Who can give me a definition of the word 'budget'?"

Johnnie: "A budget is a family quarrel."

• • •

Budget — A mathematical confirmation of your suspicion.

BUGGY

What some people drive you.

BULLETIN BOARD

In front of church: "You are not too bad to come in. You are not too good to stay out."

BULLY

I used to beat up all the kids on the block, except the McKees. I had a little trouble with them. They were boys.

BUM

Bum: Have you money for a cup of coffee, mister?

Man: No, but don't worry about me, I'll get along all right.

BUMPER-STICKER

Bumper-sticker slogan in Houston: "Be a Monkey's Uncle! Join the Zoological Society of Houston."

BURDEN

A burden which one chooses himself is not felt.

• • •

Everyone lays a burden on the willing horse.

BUS DRIVER

Definition of a school bus driver: A man who thought he liked children.

BUS FARE

Jack-in-the-box.

BUSINESS

There are two times in a man's life when he should not speculate: when he can't afford it, and when he can.   Mark Twain

• • •

Develop your business first before building your house.

• • •

Something that a lot of people give you.

• • •

He who cannot mind his own business is not to be trusted with mine.

BUSY

Whoever admits that he is too busy to improve his methods has acknowledged himself to be at the end of his rope. And that is always the saddest predicament which anyone can get into.

                    J. Ogden Armour

• • •

Have you noticed that even the busiest people are never too busy to take time to tell you how busy they are?

BUSYBODY

A person who burns the scandal at both ends.

BUTTER

Be not a baker if your head be of butter.

BUTTERFLY

Small boy to mother in curlers at dressing table: "Daddy wants to know — what time does the butterfly emerge from the cocoon."

BUY

If you buy a bad thing you will soon buy again.

BUYING

She's always forgetting. For getting this and for getting that.

CACKLING

If you would have a hen lay, you must bear with her cackling.

CAIN

Heckler: Who was Cain's wife?
Preacher: I respect any seeker of knowledge, but I want to warn you, young man, don't risk being lost to salvation by too much inquiring after other men's wives.

CALIBER

Manager of circus to human cannon ball: "You can't quit! Where will I ever find another man of your caliber?"

CALM

The calmest husbands make the stormiest wives.

•   •   •

God promises a safe landing but not a calm passage.

CAMELOT

A place where they sell used camels.

CANDIDATES

Candidates are wondering why so few folks contribute to political campaigns. Somebody should tell them we gave at the supermarket.

CANDLE

A candle loses nothing by lighting another candle.

•   •   •

Don't burn out a candle in search of a pin.

CANNIBAL

"Tell me," the missionary asked a cannibal, "do you think religion has made any headway here?"

"Yes," answered the native. "Now we eat only fishermen on Fridays."

•   •   •

Cannibal Prince: Am I too late for dinner?
Cannibal King: Yes, everybody's eaten.

CAR

Fifteen-year-old Fred: "Dad, the Bible says that if you don't let me have the car, you hate me.

Dad: "Where does it say that?"

Son: "Proverbs 13:24. He that spareth the 'rod' hateth his son."

CAR POOL

One pretty office worker to another: "So far I've had 16 car pool offers. How about you?"

CAR SICKNESS

The feeling you get every month when the payment is due.

CANOE

The difference between a Scotchman and a canoe: a canoe tips.

CASH

The vanishing American is the one who pays cash for everything he buys.

CASHIER

Banker One:	You're looking for a cashier? I thought you hired one last week.
Banker Two:	I did. That's the one we're looking for.

CATERPILLAR

Two caterpillars were crawling across the grass when they saw a butterfly flutter past above them. One nudged the other and said, "You couldn't get me up in one of those things for a million dollars!"

CATTY

A cat doesn't have nine lives but catty remarks do.

CAUCUS

The part of an animal left for the buzzards.

CAUSE

If you want to be an orator, first get your great cause.

CAUTION

It is well to swim with one foot on the ground.

●   ●   ●

Be slow of tongue and quick of eye.   Miguel de Cervantes

CEMETERY

You look like a talent scout for a cemetery.

CENSURE

I find that the pain of a little censure, even when it is unfounded, is more acute than the pleasure of much praise.

Thomas Jefferson

CENSUS

When Leif Ericson returned from his New World voyage, he found that his name had been dropped from the registry of his hometown. He reported the omission to the chief town official who, deeming it a slight to a distinguished citizen, protested strongly to the district census taker.

"I'm terribly sorry," apologized that officer in great embarrassment. "I must have taken Leif off my census."

●   ●   ●

Question:	What do they call census takers in Chinatown?
Answer:	Chinese checkers.

CHAINS

Men rattle their chains to show that they are free.

CHAIRMAN

According to Nan Hampton, a chairman of a meeting is like the minor official at a bullfight whose main function is to open and close the gates to let the bull in and out.

CHANGE

He who would be well served must know when to change his servants.

CHANNELS

God has given us two hands — one to receive with and the other to give with. We are not cisterns made for hoarding; we are channels made for sharing.

Billy Graham

CHAOS

Five women discussing the two sides of an issue.

CHAPPED

Harry: "Please give me a kiss."

Carrie: "My lips are chapped."

Harry: "Well, one more chap won't hurt them."

CHARACTER

Character is what you are in the dark.   Dwight L. Moody

• • •

Character is much easier kept than recovered.

• • •

Don't be fooled by pretty face;
Look for character and grace.

• • •

A person reveals his character by nothing so clearly as the joke he resents.

• • •

Character is not made in a crisis — it is only exhibited.

• • •

A modest pat on the back develops character, if given young enough, often enough, and low enough.

• • •

The proper time to influence the character of a child is about a hundred years before he is born.

• • •

Tears on your pillow will never wash out stains on your character.

• • •

Don't envy the lucky fellow whose path is smoothed for him. Pity him. Some day he will seek your favor. Success is the product of character. The development of your character is in your own hands, and poverty plus honest ambition is the best environment for character-building.

• • •

When wealth is lost, nothing is lost;

When health is lost, something is lost;

When character is lost, all is lost!

• • •

Character is a by-product; it is produced in the great manufacture of daily duty.

• • •

The measure of a man's real character is what he would do if he knew he would never be found out.

CHARGE

There used to be only two classes of people, but now there are three.

The haves, the have nots, and the charge-its.

CHARGED

The reason some women look so magnetic is that most everything they are wearing is charged.

CHARITY

Though I speak with the tongues of men and angels and have not charity, I am become as sounding brass, or a tinkling cymbal.

I Corinthians 13:1, KJV

CHAUVINISM

HOW TO TELL A BUSINESSMAN FROM A BUSINESSWOMAN

A businessman is dynamic; a businesswoman is aggressive.

A businessman is good on details; she is picky.

He loses his temper; she is crabby.

He's a go-getter; she is pushy.

When he's depressed, everyone tiptoes past his office;

When she is moody, it must be her time of the month.

He follows through; she doesn't know when to quit.

He's confident; she is stuck up.

He stands firm; she's hard as nails.

He has the courage of his convictions; she is stubborn.

He is a man of the world; she's been around.

He can handle his liquor; she's a lush.

He isn't afraid to say what he thinks; she's mouthy.

He's human; she's emotional.

He exercises authority diligently; she is power mad.

He is close-mouth; she is secretive.

He can make quick decisions; she's impulsive.

He's a stern taskmaster; she's hard to work for.

CHEAP

The bitterness of poor quality lingers long after the sweetness of cheap price is forgotten.

CHEAT

He that's cheated twice by the same man is an accomplice with the cheater.

•   •   •

He that will cheat at play
Will cheat you any way.

•   •   •

Bob: Did you pass your finals?
Bill: And how.
Bob: Were they easy?
Bill: Dunno...ask Jim.

CHECK

A young college student wrote home to his family: "Dear Mom and Dad: I haven't heard from you in nearly a month. Please send a check so I'll know you're all right."

CHECKING

Bridegroom: "My wife and I have a joint checking account."

Best Friend: "Isn't that hard to keep straight?

Bridegroom: "No. I put in the money and she takes it out."

CHECKBOOK

For fixing things around the house, nothing beats a man who's handy with a checkbook.

CHECK-UP

The customer brought his new car into the dealer for its 1,000 mile check-up.

"Is there anything the matter with it?" inquired the service manager.

"Well," replied the customer, "There's only one part of it that doesn't make a noise, and that's the horn."

CHEER

A cheerful heart does good like medicine, but a broken spirit makes one sick.   Proverbs 17:22

CHEERIOS

Hula-hoops for ants.

CHESS

A group of chess players had congregated in the lobby of a big New York hotel. Each person tried to outdo the other in tales of his prowess in mastering opponents. After a while, the hotel manager shouted, "Everybody out!"

Asked why, he said, "I can't stand chess nuts boasting by an open foyer.''

The Jack Carney Show, KMOX, St. Louis

CHEWING TOBACCO

New fishing lure made up of chewing tobacco. How does it work? Well, when the fish comes up to spit, you hit him with an oar.

CHILDREN

It is dangerous to confuse children with angels.

● ● ●

It is a wise child that knows his own father. Homer

● ● ●

Sam: "My daddy has a sword of Washington and a hat of Lincoln."

Bill: "My father has an Adam's apple."

● ● ●

Every couple knows how to raise the neighbor's children, so why not have all families swap children?

● ● ●

It is a wise father that knows his own child. William Shakespeare

● ● ●

If a child annoys you, quiet him by brushing his hair. If this doesn't work use the other side of the brush on the other end of the child.

● ● ●

Children are a comfort in our old age, it is true; and very often children help us reach it faster, too.

● ● ●

Mother: "Bobby, last night there were two pieces of cake in the pantry and now there is only one. How do you explain that?"

Bobby: "I guess I didn't see the other piece."

● ● ●

Satan keeps school for neglected children.

● ● ●

Father: "Why are you always at the bottom of your class?"

Dennis: "It doesn't make any difference. They teach the same thing at both ends."

● ● ●

"Billy, get your little brother's hat out of that mud puddle." "I can't ma, he's got it strapped too tight under his chin."

● ● ●

It was Washington's birthday. Johnny called over to his neighbor, Danny, "Say, aren't you going to put up your flag today?"

"Naw," answered Danny. "I don't even put the flag up for my own birthday."

● ● ●

If children did not ask questions, they would never learn how little adults know.

● ● ●

The trouble with your children is that when they're not being a lump in your throat, they're being a pain in your neck.

● ● ●

The greatest aid to adult education is children.

CHINA

"What do you think of Red China?" one lady asked another during a luncheon discussion of world affairs.

"Oh, I don't know," replied the other lady, "I guess it would be all right if you used it on a yellow tablecloth."

CHIP

A chip on the shoulder indicates there is wood higher up.

CHIPS

A man arrested for gambling came before the judge. "We weren't playing for money," he explained to the judge. "We were just playing for chips."

"Chips are just the same as money," the judge sternly replied. "I fine you fifteen dollars."

The defendant looked sad, then slowly reached into his pocket and handed the judge three blue chips.

CHOCOLATE

My wife is a lousy cook. The first time she made dinner I choked on a bone in the chocolate pudding.

CHOICE

Between two evils, choose neither; between two goods, choose both.

• • •

In literature, as in love, we are astonished at the choice made by other people.

• • •

When you have to make a choice and don't make it, that in itself is a choice.   William James

• • •

"One can decide a lot of things, but personal choices are hard. I tend to wait until one alternative is no longer available, and then inform myself that I have chosen."

CHOIR

John: What made you give up singing in the choir?

Jack: I was absent one Sunday and someone asked if the organ had been fixed.

CHOOSE

One should choose for a wife only such a woman as he would choose for a friend, were she a man.   Joubert

CHOP

"Whatever I say goes."

"Then why don't you talk about yourself for a while?"

CHRIST

Christ sends none away empty but those who are full of themselves.

• • •

Christ never wrote a tract, but He went about doing good.

CHRISTIAN

Christian names are everywhere; Christian men are very rare.

• • •

Nobody can teach you how to be a Christian — you learn it on the job.

CHRISTIANITY

The trouble with some of us is that we have been inoculated with small doses of Christianity which keeps us from catching the real thing.

• • •

If a man cannot be a Christian in the place where he is, he cannot be a Christian anywhere.

Henry Ward Beecher

• • •

There is one single fact which we may oppose to all the wit and argument of infidelity, namely, that no man ever repented of being a Christian on his death bed.

• • •

Christianity has not been tried and found wanting; it has been found difficult and not tried.
Chesterton

• • •

Christian: one who believes that the New Testament is a divinely inspired book admirably suited to the spiritual needs of his neighbors.

• • •

Christianity is bread for daily, use, not cake for special occasions.

CHRISTMAS

Many a Christmas tie is in a clash by itself.
Bob Orben

• • •

Anyone who thinks Christmas doesn't last all year doesn't have a charge account.

• • •

At Christmas, the kids would like something that will separate the men from the toys.

• • •

This Christmas I'm giving my wife something worth $50 — a $100 bill!

• • •

"For Christmas," a woman remarked to her friend, "I was visited by a jolly, bearded fellow with a big bag over his shoulder. My son came from college with his laundry."

• • •

Christmas began in the heart of God. It is complete only when it reaches the heart of man.

• • •

It is good to be children sometimes, and never better than at Christmas, when its mighty Founder was a child himself.
Dickens

• • •

Department store sign: Keep Christmas with you all year — use our monthly payment plan.

• • •

There seems to be some question as to whether more gifts are exchanged on Christmas or the day after.

CHURCH

A place where you encounter nodding acquaintances.

• • •

Every church has in addition to the brakeman, a construction and wrecking crew. To which do you belong? One of them SURE.

• • •

Many bring their clothes to church rather than themselves.

• • •

Some people go to church to see who didn't.

• • •

"Join our sit-in demonstration every Sunday."

• • •

The chief trouble with the church is that you and I are in it.

• • •

Some go to church to take a walk;
Some go there to laugh and talk;
Some go there to meet a friend;
Some go there their time to spend;
Some go there to meet a lover;
Some go there a fault to cover;
Some go there for speculation;

Some go there for observation;
Some go there to doze and nod;
The wise go there to worship God.

CHURCH BULLETIN BOARDS

Come in and have your faith lifted.

Come in and let us prepare you for your finals.

A miser is a rich pauper.

Ask about our pray-as-you-go plan

We hold sit-in demonstrations every Sunday.

No matter how much you nurse a grudge it won't get better.

Start living to beat hell.

If some people lived up to their ideals they would be stooping.

Everything you always wanted to know about heaven and hell but were afraid to ask.

Pray up in advance.

Patience is the ability to stand something as long as it happens to the other fellow.

Think twice before you speak and you may say something even more aggravating.

CIGARETTE

A political prisoner was about to be executed by the new dictatorial regime. He was blindfolded by the captain of the firing squad and asked if he wanted a cigarette.

"No thank you," said the prisoner. "I'm trying to quit."

CITIZENS

Whatever makes men good Christians, makes them good citizens.   Daniel Webster

CITIZENSHIP

Voting is the least arduous of a citizen's duties. He has the prior and harder duty of making up his mind.

CIVILIZATION

After several thousand years, civilization has progressed to a point where we lock all our doors and windows every night while jungle natives sleep in open huts.

CLAMDIGGER

A person who is mussel bound.

CLASS

All mankind is divided into three classes: those that are immovable, those that are movable, and those that move.

CLASSICS

The classics are something somebody praises and nobody reads.

CLEANLINESS

Cleanliness is next to impossible.

•   •   •

Cleanliness is next to Godliness, but in childhood it's next to impossible.

CLERGYMAN

Clergyman: I've lost my brief-case.
Traveller: I pity your grief.
Clergyman: My sermons are in it.
Traveller: I pity the thief.

CLEVER

Do clever men make good husbands? Clever men don't become husbands.

CLEVERNESS

Find enough clever things to say, and you're a Prime Minister; write them down and you're Shakespeare.   George Bernard Shaw

CLIMB

He who climbs too high may have a fall;

But better a fall than not climb at all.

CLIMBING

To keep from falling, keep climbing.

CLOTHES

Teenager, Mary, was in tears the other night because she had nothing to wear for her date. All her sweat shirts were in the wash.

CLOVERLEAF

There is a growing sentiment that the national flower should be a concrete cloverleaf.

COACH

A coach was being congratulated on having a lifetime contract. "I guess it's all right," he said. "But I remember another guy with a lifetime contract. Had a bad year, and the president called him in, pronounced him dead and fired him."

COFFEE

They serve blended coffee — today's and yesterday's.

●   ●   ●

A man went into a restaurant and said: "I want a cup of coffee without cream."

The waitress came back in a few minutes and said, "I am sorry, Sir, but we are all out of cream. Would you mind taking your coffee without milk?"

COFFIN

My brother has invented a new coffin. It just goes over the head. It's for people who are dead from the neck up. Do you want to buy one?

COINCIDE

What most people do when it rains.

COLD

Question: Which travels faster ...heat or cold?

Answer: Heat...because you can catch cold easily.

COLDCUT

Buck: Were you ever married?

Glen: Yeh, but my wife ran away.

Buck: How did it happen?

Glen: She ran away when I was taking a bath.

Buck: I'll bet she waited years for the opportunity.

COLLECTION

A church function in which many people take only a passing interest.

COLLEGE

Today when you hear about a college three-letter man, you wonder if it's LSD or POT!

●   ●   ●

Most college campuses are getting so crowded that if a student wants to be alone he has to go to class!

●   ●   ●

College never hurt a man — unless, of course, he happened to be the student's father....

●   ●   ●

"Has your son's college education been of any tangible value?" inquired a friend.

"Oh yes...for one thing, it completely cured his mother of bragging about him."

●   ●   ●

A father passing through his sons college town late one evening on a business trip, thought he would pay him a surprise visit. Arriving at the fraternity house he rapped loudly on the door. After several minutes of knocking a sleepy voice from the second floor window asked, ''Whaddyah want?''

''Does Clyde Foster live here?'' asked the father.

''Yeh,'' replied the voice. ''Just dump him on the front porch.''

• • •

The young man had just graduated from college and went to work in the family store. The first day his father asked him to sweep the sidewalk.

''But, Dad,'' he protested, ''I'm a college graduate.''

''I forgot about that,'' replied his father, ''But don't worry, I'll show you how.''

• • •

Dad doesn't waste words when he writes a letter. One he sent to me at Simmons College was enclosed with air fare home for Christmas vacation. The letter read: ''Dear Sue, Here's some bread so you can get back to the breadbox.''

• • •

Gal: And just why did you have to cut in while I was dancing with a four-letter man? You're just a freshman.

Guy: I'm sorry, ma'am, but I'm working my way through college and your partner was waving a five-dollar bill at me.

• • •

Freshman: I don't know.
Sophomore: I'm not prepared.
Junior: I don't remember.
Senior: I don't believe I can add anything to what has already been said.

• • •

Father: My son just received his B.A.
Neighbor: I suppose now he'll be looking for a Ph.D.
Father: No, now he's looking for a J-O-B.

• • •

My son went to college and received an M.A. and a B.A. but his P.A. still supports him.

• • •

Letter from son at school:
Dear Dad,
Gue$$ what I need mo$t. That'$ right. $end it $oon.
Be$t Wi$he$
Jay

Reply:
Dear Jay,
NOthing ever happens here. We kNOw you like school. Write aNOther letter soon. Mom was asking about you at NOon.
NOw I have to say good-by,
Dad

COLLEGE-BRED
A four-year loaf made with father's dough.

COLLEGE-CHEER
The check from home.

COLONEL SANDERS
A farmer vows he increased egg production by putting this sign in the henhouse: ''An egg a day keeps Colonel Sanders away.''

COMEBACK

Farmer: What are you doing in that tree, young man?

Boy: One of your apples fell down and I'm putting it back.

COMEDIAN

A person who has a good memory for old jokes.

COMFORT

No man's head aches while he comforts another.

COMPANIONS

Only an ass will bray at an ass.

• • •

Bad company is like a nail driven into a post, which, after the first or second blow, may be drawn out with little difficulty; but being once driven up to the head, the pincers cannot take hold to draw it out, but which can only be done by the destruction of the wood.

Augustine

• • •

A man among children, a child becomes; a child among men, a man.

• • •

Be with wise men and become wise. Be with evil men and become evil.

• • •

He that lies with dogs rises with fleas.

• • •

Keep good company, and you will be of the number. But if you keep company with bad men, their number will soon be increased by one.

• • •

Keep company with good men, and you'll increase their number.

COMPARTMENT

One woman to another: "My purse has a compartment I call the Bermuda Triangle. Items from other compartments drop into it and disappear."

COMPETITION

The reason why men who mind their own business succeed is because they have so little competition.

COMPLAINT

The wheel that squeaks the loudest is the first to be replaced.

• • •

The wheel that squeaks the loudest is the one that gets the grease. Josh Billings

• • •

Waiter: We haven't had a complaint in twenty-five years.

Customer: No wonder. The customers all starve to death before they are served.

COMPLAINING

Better to live in the desert than with a quarrelsome, complaining woman. Proverbs 21:19

COMPLIMENT

I have been complimented many times and they always embarrass me; I always feel that they have not said enough. Mark Twain

• • •

Whenever a man's friends begin to compliment him about looking young, he may be sure that they think he is growing old.

Washington Irving

COMPROMISE

Colonel Compromise is the best and cheapest lawyer.

• • •

If a godly man compromises with the wicked, it is like polluting a fountain or muddying a spring.

Proverbs 25:26

COMPUTER

If computers get too powerful, we can organize them into committies. That'll do them in.

• • •

To err is human; to really foul things up requires a computer.

COSMETICS

According to historians women used cosmetics in the Middle Ages...and today women are using cosmetics in the middle ages too.

COMMAND

He who can commands, and he who will obeys.

COMMERCIALS

Television commercials are the pause that depresses.

COMMITTEE

A committee is a group that keeps minutes and loses hours.

Milton Berle

• • •

To get something done a committee should consist of three men, two of whom are absent.

• • •

If you want to kill any idea in the world today, get a committee working on it.

• • •

Never fear that machines may get too powerful. When they do, we can organize them into committees.

• • •

A committee is a group of people who talk for hours to produce a result called minutes.

• • •

Committee is a noun of multitude, signifying many, but not signifying much.

COMMON BOND

The common bond of rebels is their guilt. The common bond of godly people is good will.

COMMON SENSE

Common sense is very uncommon.   Horace Greeley

• • •

Common sense is the knack of seeing things as they are, and doing things as they ought to be done.   Josh Billings

• • •

Common sense is only a modification of talent. Genius is an exaltation of it. The difference is, therefore, in degree, not nature.

• • •

Common sense is not so common.

• • •

Have two goals: wisdom — that is, knowing and doing right — and common sense. Don't let them slip away, for they fill you with living energy, and are a feather in your cap. They keep you safe from defeat and disaster and from stumbling off the trail. With them on guard you can sleep without fear; you need not be afraid of disaster or the plots of wicked men; for the Lord is with you; He protects you.   Proverbs 3:21-26

• • •

The man who strays away from common sense will end up dead!

COMMONWEALTH

A joint checking account.

COMMUNICATION

I know you believe you understand what you think I said, but I'm not sure you realize that what you heard is not what I meant.

COMMUNISM

Communism has nothing to do with love. Communism is an excellent hammer which we use to destroy our enemy.   Mao Tse-tung

• • •

A communist is like a crocodile: when it opens its mouth you cannot tell whether it is trying to smile or preparing to eat you up.

Winston Churchill

• • •

The theory of Communism may be summed up in one sentence: Abolish all private property.

Karl Marx

CONCEAL

He's a fool that cannot conceal his wisdom.

CONCEIT

Conceit is God's gift to little men.

• • •

A person who suffers from too much vitamin I in his system.

• • •

We like the person who tells us all the nice things about ourselves that we always knew.

• • •

Executive to colleague: "Well, no, I wouldn't say he's conceited; but he's absolutely convinced that if he hadn't been born people would want to know why."

CONCLUSION

The troops were being taught to jump from a plane.

"What if my parachute doesn't open?" asked one rookie.

"That," said the instructor, "is known as jumping to a conclusion."

• • •

Jumping at conclusions is not half as good exercise as digging for facts.

• • •

A doctor, appearing as an expert witness on behalf of a man injured in a car accident, was being badgered by an overbearing attorney.

"You say, Doctor, that you're familiar with symptoms of brain concussion?"

"That's correct," replied the Doctor.

"Well tell me, Doctor," continued the attorney; "If you and I were riding in a car, and another car struck us and our heads bumped together, is it your opinion that we would suffer concussion?"

"It's my opinion," replied the Doctor, "that I would and you wouldn't."

CONDEMN

You can't hold a man down without staying down with him.

Booker T. Washington

CONFERENCE

An experienced executive said it, "A conference is the confusion of one man multiplied by the number present."

CONFESSOR

It's a foolish sheep that makes the wolf his confessor.

CONFESSION

The confession of evil works is the first beginning of good works.
St. Augustine

• • •

Confession is the first step to repentance.

CONFIDENCE

Confidence of success is almost success.

CONGRESSMEN

Put all our Congressmen together and they weigh about 96,000 pounds. It's hard to get anything that weighs 48 tons to move quickly.

CONNECTIONS

Many a live wire would be dead without connections.

CONSCIENCE

He who sacrifices his conscience to ambition burns a picture to obtain the ashes.

• • •

The still, small voice that warns us that someone is watching.

• • •

Small boy's definition of conscience: "Something that makes you tell your mother before your sister does."

• • •

A conscience, like a buzzing bee, can make a fellow uneasy without ever stinging him.

• • •

A clear conscience is a soft pillow.

• • •

A national conscience is a still small voice that tells one country when another country is stronger.

• • •

When a person feels that his thinking is getting broader, it is more likely that his conscience is stretching.

• • •

My conscience hath a thousand several tongues.   Shakespeare

• • •

Conscience doesn't keep you from doing anything; it just keeps you from enjoying it.

• • •

Conscience is what hurts when everything else feels so good.

• • •

A good conscience is a continual Christmas.   Benjamin Franklin

• • •

Keep conscience clear, then never fear.

• • •

A man's conscience is the Lord's searchlight exposing his hidden motives.   Proverbs 20:27

CONSERVATIVE

No man can be a conservative until he has something to lose.

CONSISTENT

The only advice I get about raising children is to be consistent. But how can I be consistent? They never do the same thing twice.

CONTENTED

Who is wise? He that learns from everyone.
Who is powerful? He that governs the passions.
Who is rich? He that is content.
Who is that? Nobody.

• •

Our idea of a contented man is the one, if any, that enjoys the scenery along the detour.

•   •   •

A contented mind is a continual feast.

CONVENTION

Where people pass a lot of resolutions but few bars.

CONVERSATION

A man's conversation is the mirror of his thoughts.

•   •   •

When there is a gap in the conversation, don't put your foot in it.

CONVERTED

You have not converted a man because you have silenced him.

CONVICTION

The difference between conviction and prejudice is that you can explain a conviction without getting angry.

COOK

Bride: "The two best things I cook are meatloaf and apple dumplings."

Groom: "Well, which is this?"

COOKS

God sends us good meat, but the devil sends us cooks.

COOKIES

Wife: I baked two kinds of cookies today. Would you like to take your pick?

Husband: No thanks. I'll use my hammer.

COMPETITION

Two barber shops were in red hot competition. One put up a sign advertising haircuts for 75 cents. His competitor put up one that read, "We repair 75 cent haircuts."

COPING

Perhaps one way of coping with the population explosion would be to give every potential parent some experience in driving a school bus.

CONQUER

Conquer a dog before you contend with a lion.

COOPERATION

An old ferryman painted the word "Faith" on one oar and "Works" on the other. When asked the reason he explained: "To make a passage across the river you need both oars. See where 'Faith' without 'Works' takes us." The ferryman slipped one oar and turned with "Faith" only, and went around and around in a circle. "Now let us try 'Works' without 'Faith.' We make just a little headway; and it is just the same in the journey of life."

CORNS

As we grow older we don't feel our oats half as much as our corns.

CORRESPONDENCE

"Mary, where did you learn to sing?"

"I graduated from correspondence school."

"You must have missed a lot of mail."

CORRUPTION

When you remove dross from silver, you have sterling ready for the silversmith. When you remove corrupt men from the king's court, his reign will be just and fair.

Proverbs 25:4-5

COUNTERFEITER

...The part-time counterfeiter who ran an after-dinner mint?

COUNTERSIGN

Unless you have the extra cash on hand, don't countersign a note. Why risk everything you own? They'll even take your bed!

Proverbs 22:26-27

COUNTRY

"What could be more sad," mused the sentimental professor, "than a man without a country?"

"A country without a man," answered the pretty girl.

COURT

...A place where they dispense with justice.

• • •

The penalty for laughing in a courtroom is six months in jail; if it were not for this penalty, the jury would never hear the evidence.

COURTEOUS

No man is too big to be courteous, but some are too little.

COUNSEL

Too much taking counsel ends in doing nothing.

• • •

In great straits and when hope is small, the boldest counsels are the safest.

COUNSELORS

Don't go to war without wise guidance; there is safety in many counselors. Proverbs 24:6

• • •

Plans go wrong with too few counselors; many counselors bring success. Proverbs 15:22

COUNTENANCE

A happy face means a glad heart; a sad face means a breaking heart. Proverbs 15:13

COURAGE

Give us the fortitude to endure the things which cannot be changed, and the courage to change the things which should be changed, and the wisdom to know one from the other.

• • •

Last, but by no means least, courage — moral courage, the courage of one's convictions, the courage to see things through. The world is in a constant conspiracy against the brave. It's the age-old struggle — the roar of the crowd on one side and the voice of your conscience on the other.

Douglas MacArthur

• • •

A man's courage can sustain his broken body, but when courage dies, what hope is left?

Proverbs 18:14

• • •

One man with courage makes a majority. Andrew Jackson

COURTESY

We must be as courteous to a man as we are to a picture, which we are willing to give the advantage of a good light.

Ralph Waldo Emerson

COURTING

In the old days the young fellow who went courting turned down the gas. Now he steps on it.

COURTSHIP

A courtship begins when a man whispers sweet nothings, and ends when he says nothing sweet.

• • •

In courtship a man pursues a woman until she catches him.

• • •

Every young man knows when the right girl comes along because she tells him.

• • •

A young man had been courting a girl for quite some time, and trying to no avail to get her consent to marriage. He finally confided to her that "my elderly father is quite sickly and will probably die soon. When that happens I will be a millionaire."

Two days later she became his stepmother.

COVETOUS

The covetous man is ever in want.

COVETOUSNESS

Covetousness is the punishment of the rich.

COW

Frank: "You must have had a terrible accident last night. The front of your car is all smashed in. What did you hit?"

Hank: "Last night I was driving and hit a cow..."

Frank: "A Jersey cow?"

Hank: "I don't know — I didn't see her license plate."

COWARD

A hundred times in life a coward dies.

COWARDICE

Cowards die many times before their deaths; the valiant never taste of death but once.
                    William Shakespeare

• • •

Every hard-boiled egg is yellow inside.

• • •

There are several good protections against temptation, but the surest is cowardice.   Mark Twain

C. P. N.

Myrlene: He's a C.P.N.

Sharon: You mean C.P.A. Certified Public Accountant.

Myrlene: No... C.P.N. Constant Pain in the Neck.

CRABBY

It is better to live in the corner of an attic than with a crabby woman in a lovely home.   Proverbs 21:9

CRANKY

A constant dripping on a rainy day and a cranky woman are much alike! You can no more stop her complaints than you can stop the wind or hold onto anything with oil-slick hands.   Proverbs 27:15

CRAZY

What a joke book writer is.

CREASE

When packing vacation clothes, take the line of crease resistance.

CREATIVE

The award for the most original and creative script went to a TV series that was based on a hit movie version of a Broadway play adapted from a best-selling novel that follows a classic Shakespearean theme.

CREDIT

The world's poorest credit risk is the man who agrees to pay a stranger's debts.　　Proverbs 27:13

•　　•　　•

Credit is like chastity, they can both stand temptation better than suspicion.　　Josh Billings

•　　•　　•

No man's credit is as good as his money.

•　　•　　•

Be sure you know a person well before you vouch for his credit! Better refuse than suffer later.
　　　　　　Proverbs 11:15

•　　•　　•

The surest way to establish your credit is to work yourself into the position of not needing any.

•　　•　　•

The man had barely paid off his mortgage on the house when he mortgaged it again to buy a car and, not long after, he borrowed money to build a garage. His banker hesitated, and said, "If I do make this new loan, how will you buy gas for the car?"

"It seems to me," replied the borrower curtly, "that a fellow who owns a big house, a car and garage should be able to get credit for gasoline."

•　　•　　•

Glen: Are you still living within your income?
Rich: No. It's all I can do to live within my credit.

CREDULITY

The great masses of the people... will more easily fall victims to a great lie than to a small one.
　　　　　　Adolf Hitler

CRIME

Set a thief to catch a thief.

•　　•　　•

Few men have virtue to withstand the highest bidder.
　　　　　　George Washington

•　　•　　•

We don't seem to be able to check crime, so why not legalize it and then tax it out of business.
　　　　　　Will Rogers

CRIMINAL

One who gets caught.

CRISIS

Man is not imprisoned by habit. Great changes in him can be wrought by crisis—once that crisis can be recognized and understood.

• • •

A friend is going through an identity crisis and an energy crisis at the same time. He doesn't know who he is, and he's too tired to find out.

CRITIC

He who sows thorns should not go barefoot.

• • •

A wet blanket that soaks everything it touches.

• • •

Critic's comment about a play: The scenery was beautiful, but the actors got in front of it.

• • •

Pay no attention to what critics say. There has never been a statue set up in honor of a critic.

CRITICIZE

Criticize by creating.
Michelangelo

CRITICISM

The trouble with most of us is that we would rather be ruined by praise than saved by criticism.

• • •

Don't refuse to accept criticism; get all the help you can.
Proverbs 23:12

• • •

It is a badge of honor to accept valid criticism.   Proverbs 25:12

• • •

If you refuse criticism you will end in poverty and disgrace; if you accept criticism you are on the road to fame.   Proverbs 13:18

• • •

No one so thoroughly appreciates the value of constructive criticism as the one who's giving it.

• • •

The public is the only critic whose opinion is worth anything at all.   Mark Twain

• • •

Criticism, as it was first instituted by Aristotle, was meant as a standard of judging well.
Samuel Johnson

• • •

Remember that nobody will ever get ahead of you as long as he is kicking you in the seat of the pants.   Walter Winchell

• • •

Even the lion has to defend himself against flies.

• • •

To avoid criticism do nothing, say nothing, be nothing.

• • •

The strength of criticism lies only in the weakness of the thing criticized   Longfellow

• • •

When some people abuse you, they can't understand why you resent "constructive criticism."

• • •

When someone says, "I do not wish to appear critical," it means he is going to let you have it.

• • •

Heat hardens clay, but melts wax. It tempers steel but softens lead. The hot sun ripens fruit and grain, but withers and blasts the cut flowers and tender plants. Wintry blasts work havoc with summer annuals, but toughen the fiber of the mighty oaks. The difference in results is not with the external agent but with the inherent qualities of the receiving object.

Every person who attempts to do anything worthwhile has to learn to take criticism, constructive or otherwise. Often those who accomplish most in the long run come in for the most criticism.

CROOKED

Many make straight things crooked, but few make crooked things straight.

CROSSWORD PUZZLE

Did you hear about the crossword puzzle addict who died and was buried six feet down and three across?

CROW

That is a sad house where the hen crows louder than the cock.

• • •

A scolding wife and crowing hen, I could not wish to hear again.

• • •

A rooster crows early in the morning because he probably can't get in a word after the hens get up.

CRUEL

One of the ill effects of cruelty is that it makes the bystanders cruel.

CRY

If at first you don't succeed, cry, cry again.

CRYOGENICS

What's so new about cryogenics, the science of freezing bodies? My landlord does it every winter.

CUBIC

Question: What is a cubic?
Answer: The language spoken in Cuba.

CUCKOO

"Is your husband very good at fixing things around the house?"

"Well, I don't like to criticize, but ever since he fixed the clock, the cuckoo backs out and asks, 'What time is it?'"

CULTURE

The man had been dragged to a classical violin concert by his culture-minded wife. Trying to teach him some of the finer points she whispered during the concert, "What do you think of his execution?"

"I'm all for it," replied the husband.

CUNNING

Cunning is a short blanket — if you pull it over your face, you expose your feet.

CUPID

Cupid's darts hurt more coming out than going in.

CURE

The first step toward cure is to know what the disease is.

CURIOSITY

You know what a woman's curiosity is. Almost as great as a man's.

* * *

The important thing is not to stop questioning. Curiosity has its own reason for existing. One cannot help but be in awe when he contemplates the mysteries of eternity, of life, of the marvelous structure of reality. It is enough if one tries merely to comprehend a little of this mystery every day. Never lose a holy curiosity.

Albert Einstein

CURRENT

It takes a strong man to swim against the current; and dead fish will float with it.

CURSES

Curses, like young chickens, still come home to roost.

CYNIC

A cynic is a man who, when he smells flowers, looks around for a coffin.

* * *

One who is married.

* * *

A cynic is a man who knows the price of everything, and the value of nothing.   Oscar Wilde

DADDY

Every male parent is a daddy, but not every daddy is a male parent.

Mother: Did you enjoy your ride in the car with Daddy?

Little
Daughter: Oh, yes. It was lots of fun. We saw lots and lots of darn fools, and I don't know how many boneheads.

DAMP

Pam: Why was your letter so damp?
Rosie: Postage due, I guess.

DANCE

Rod: I'm through with that girl.
Doug: Oh, why?
Rod: She asked me if I danced.
Doug: Well, what's wrong with that?
Rod: I was dancing with her when she asked me.

DANDELION

Question: What is another name for pretty good fibbing?
Answer: Dandelion.

DANDRUFF

Small, whitish scales trying to get ahead.

DANGER

There's nothing so comfortable as a small bankroll; a big one is always in danger.   Wilson Mizner

Anger is only one letter short of danger.

Facing danger is not courage unless one knows the danger faced.

DATING

"Excuse me for bothering you coming to the door for your daughter," apologized the young man, "but my horn isn't working."

Guy: Hello, Lisa, do you still love me?
Gal: Lisa? My name is Roberta.
Guy: I'm so sorry...I keep thinking this is Thursday.

DAY

I'd enjoy the day more if it started later.

One of these days is none of these days.

What a day may bring, a day may take away.

DEAD

"Do you believe it is possible to communicate with the dead?"

"Yes, I can hear you distinctly."

DEATH

There'll be many a dry eye at his death.

● ● ●

Is death the last sleep? No, it is the last and final awakening.

Sir Walter Scott

DEAF

None so deaf as those that will not hear. Matthew Henry

DEAF AND DUMB

She talks so much she was married three years before she found out that her husband was deaf and dumb.

● ● ●

Did you hear about the deaf and dumb guy who wore boxing gloves to bed so he wouldn't talk in his sleep.

DEAF MUTE

Did you hear about the deaf mute boy who used so many dirty words that his mother washed his hands with soap and water.

DEAFNESS

A scientist claims that loud rock music is beneficial in some cases of deafness. But, then, deafness is beneficial in some cases of rock music.

DEAR JOHN

One of Joe's bunk-mates broke up with his girlfriend. The girl-friend wrote demanding that he return her photograph immediate-ly. The soldier borrowed a collec-tion of several pictures of various girls and sent them to his ex-sweet-heart with her photo tucked in among them. He enclosed a note:

"Dear Mildred, pick out yours. I have forgotten what you look like."

DEBT

A man in debt is so far a slave.

Ralph Waldo Emerson

● ● ●

Some debts are fun when you are acquiring them, but none are fun when you set about retiring them. Ogden Nash

● ● ●

Debt is the slavery of the free.

● ● ●

Falsehood follows at the heels of debt.

● ● ●

Don't withhold repayment of your debts. Don't say, "Some other time," if you can pay now.

Proverbs 3:27-28

● ● ●

It is poor judgment to counter-sign another's note, to become responsible for his debts.

Proverbs 17:18

DECISIONS

One moment may throw down the credit years have built.

● ● ●

Did you hear about the parents who sent their young son to camp to learn to make decisions of his own?

He did. The second day there he decided to come home.

DECEIT

It is double the pleasure to deceive the deceiver.

● ● ●

Every crowd has a silver lining.
P. T. Barnum

• • •

You can fool some of the people all the time, and all of the people some of the time, but you cannot fool all of the people all the time.
Abraham Lincoln

• • •

Question: What is deceit?
Answer: A place to sit.

DECEIVE

Oh, what a tangled web we weave,
When first we practice to deceive.
Scott

• • •

The greatest deceiver — one who deceives himself.

• • •

Oh, what a tangled web we weave,
When once we venture to deceive!

• • •

R.D.: She said I'm interesting, brave and intelligent.
Bob: You should never go steady with a girl who deceives you from the very start.

DECORATION DAY

What some people think Easter Sunday is.

DEEDS

Small deeds done are better than great deeds planned. Peter Marshall

• • •

A man of words and not of deeds
Is like a garden full of weeds.

• • •

Many prayers remain unanswered, pending endorsement of our deeds.

• • •

The smallest deed is better than the grandest intention.

• • •

Charm can be deceptive and beauty doesn't last, but a woman who fears and reverences God shall be greatly praised. Praise her for the many fine things she does. These good deeds of hers shall bring her honor and recognition from even the leaders of the nation.
Proverbs 31:30-31

DEFEAT

Defeat isn't bitter if you don't swallow it.

• • •

Believe you are defeated, believe it long enough, and it is likely to become a fact.
Norman Vincent Peale

• • •

Politics have become so expensive that it takes a lot of money even to be defeated.
Will Rogers

DEFENDANT

"You have known the defendant how long?"
"Twelve years."
"Tell the court whether you think he is the type of man who would steal this money or not."
"How much was it?"

DEFINITIONS

Daffy definitions from Sunkist School second graders: "An island is a whole lot of water with a little dirt in it." "Quiet is when there isn't 'enebode' saying 'enething.' "

"Washington is the last name of the first president of the U.S." "A gem is a place where you play ball sometimes."

DELINQUENT

When adults act like children, they're silly; when children act like adults, they are delinquent.

DEMOCRACY

In free countries, every man is entitled to express his opinions — and every other man is entitled not to listen.

• • •

Democracy is the art and science of running the circus from the monkey cage.

DENSE

Teacher: "What are the people of New York noted for?"

Charlie: "For their stupidity."

Teacher: "Where ever did you get that idea?"

Charlie: "It says here in this book that the population of New York is very dense."

DENTIST

One who lives from hand to mouth.

• • •

A person you see when your toothache drives you to extraction.

• • •

Upon receiving the bill for the extraction of a tooth, the patient phoned his dentist to complain that, "that's three times what you normally charge!"

"Yes, I know," replied the dentist, "But you yelled so loud you scared away two other patients."

• • •

Dentist: Stop making faces. I haven't even touched you yet!

Patient: I know you haven't. . . but you're standing on my foot.

• • •

Patient: Hey, that wasn't the tooth I wanted pulled.

Dentist: Calm yourself, I'm coming to it!

• • •

Woman to dentist who talked constantly: Will you please stop talking so I can concentrate on my pain.

• • •

Esther: Did you have a good time at the dentist's?

Melba: I was bored to tears.

DEPRESSION

Depressions may bring people closer to the church — but so do funerals.

DERMATOLOGIST

Dermatologists make rash judgments.

DESERVE

It is better to deserve without receiving, than to receive without deserving.

DESIRE

There are two tragedies in life. One is not get your heart's desire. The other is to get it.

George Bernard Shaw

• • •

The reason so few people get what they want is because they don't want hard enough.

If you desire many things, many things will seem but a few.

Lord, grant that I may always desire more than I can accomplish.
Michelangelo

DESK
A wastebasket with drawers.

DESPERATION
The burglar stuck a gun in the man's back but the man turned suddenly, applied a judo grip and flung him across the alley. Then he pounced on the burglar and began to wipe him out. He blackened his eyes, broke his jaw, fractured his ribs and broke his arm. Finally the crook cried in desperation, "Hey, mister, ain't you never gonna call a cop?"

DETERMINATION
Beware of what you set your mind on for that you will surely become.
Emerson

No termination without determination.

DEVIL
Talk of the devil, and his horns appear, says the proverb.
Samuel Taylor Coleridge

Resist the devil, and he will flee from you.
James 4:7, KJV

For where God built a church, there the Devil would also build a chapel.
Martin Luther

Don't open the door when the Devil looks in at the window.

Why do I believe in the Devil? For three reasons:
1. Because the Bible plainly says he exists.
2. Because I see his work everywhere.
3. Because great scholars have recognized his existence.
Billy Graham

DIARY
"I wouldn't want to say my wife always gets her own way," said a man to his neighbor, "But she writes her diary a week ahead of time."

DICE
The best throw of the dice is to throw them away.

DICTATOR
"Do you know who the greatest dictator in the world is?"
"Know her...I married her!"

DIE
It's not that I'm afraid to die. I just don't want to be there when it happens.

Bob: Darling, I could die for your sake.
Esther: You are always saying that, but you never do it.

DIET
The best way to lose weight is to eat all you want of everything you don't like.

A diet is what helps a person gain weight more slowly.

• • •

Diets are recommended for those who are thick and tired of it.

DIFFERENCE

"She's good-looking" and "she's looking good" is about 20 years and 30 pounds.

• • •

The difference between the right word and the almost right word is the difference between lightning and lightning bug.   Mark Twain

DIFFICULTY

The occasion is piled high with difficulty, and we must rise high with the occasion.   Lincoln

• • •

Looking difficulty squarely in the face will often kill it.

• • •

There are two ways of meeting difficulties: you alter the difficulties or you alter yourself meeting them.

DIG

He who wants to dig will find a spade somewhere.

DILIGENCE

The expectations of life depend upon diligence; the mechanic that would perfect his work must first sharpen his tools.

DIMPLE

Is that a dimple, or did the hole in your head slip?

DINNER

A good dinner sharpens wit, while it softens the heart.

DIPLOMACY

A diplomat is a man who remembers a lady's birthday but forgets her age.

• • •

Modern diplomats approach every problem with an open mouth.

• • •

Diplomacy is the art of letting someone have your way.

• • •

Diplomacy: lying in state.

DIPLOMAT

A diplomat is a man who says you have an open mind instead of telling you that you have a hole in your head.

• • •

One who never heard that old joke before.

DIRECTION

To know the road ahead ask those coming back.

• • •

The world turns aside to let any man pass who knows whither he is going.   David Starr Jordan

• • •

Since the Lord is directing our steps, why try to understand everything that happens along the way?   Proverbs 20:24

• • •

Before every man there lies a wide and pleasant road that seems right but ends in death.
                    Proverbs 14:12

DIRT

He who falls in the dirt, the longer he lies the dirtier he is.

DISAGREE

Man to friend: "By the time I found out my father was right, my son was old enough to disagree with me."

• • •

Wife: I'm afraid the mountain air would disagree with me.

Husband: My dear, it wouldn't dare.

DISAPPOINTED

Most persons who get something for nothing are disappointed if they don't get more.

DISAPPOINTMENT

Too many people miss the silver lining because they're expecting gold.

DISAPPROVAL

There are few people who are more often in the wrong than those who cannot endure to be thought so. Francois de La Rochefoucauld

DISCIPLINE

Discipline doesn't break a child's spirit half as often as the lack of it breaks a parent's heart.

• • •

Bending a youngster over is sometimes a good way of straightening him out!

• • •

Eight-year-old boy's description of mother's punishment procedure: "After the storm comes a palm!"

• • •

At last we've discovered how to get the children to bed without arguments. Let them stay up as late as they want.

• • •

You never will be the person you can be if pressure, tension, and discipline are taken out of your life.

• • •

If you refuse to discipline your son, it proves you don't love him; for if you love him you will be prompt to punish him.
Proverbs 13:24

• • •

Discipline your son in his early years while there is hope. If you don't you will ruin his life.
Proverbs 19:18

• • •

A youngster's heart is filled with rebellion, but punishment will drive it out of him. Proverbs 22:15

• • •

Don't fail to correct your children; discipline won't hurt them! They won't die if you use a stick on them! Punishment will keep them out of hell. Proverbs 23:13-14

• • •

Scolding and spanking a child helps him to learn. Left to himself, he brings shame to his mother.
Proverbs 29:15

• • •

Discipline your son and he will give you happiness and peace of mind. Proverbs 29:17

• • •

Discipline, like the bridle in the hand of a good rider, should exercise its influence without appearing to do so; should be ever active, both as a support and as a restraint, yet seem to lie easily in hand. It must always be ready to check or to pull up, as occasion may require; and only when the horse is a runaway should the action of the curb be perceptible.

• • •

Becky: I see your father raised you properly.

Dave: Raised me? He used to raise me a foot off the floor when he raised me.

• • •

A permissive mother said to her wild little son, "Sit down and stop making so much noise."

"No, I won't...so there!" said the boy in an impudent tone.

"Stand up, then...I will be obeyed!"

• • •

Rearing children these days is like drafting a blueprint: you have to know where to draw the line.

DISCONTENT

Discontent is something that follows ambition like a shadow.

• • •

One thing only has been lent to youth and age in common — discontent.   Matthew Arnold

DISCRETION

An ounce of discretion is worth a pound of learning.

• •

Make your affairs known in the marketplace, and one will call them black and another white.

• • •

As a jewel of gold in a swine's snout, so is a fair woman which is without discretion.

• • •

If you shout a pleasant greeting to a friend too early in the morning, he will count it as a curse!   Proverbs 27:14

DISCUSS

Small minds discuss persons.
Average minds discuss events.
Great minds discuss ideas.

• • •

Great minds discuss ideas, average minds discuss events, small minds discuss people.

DISCUSSION

A friendly discussion is as stimulating as the sparks that fly when iron strikes iron.
                                Proverbs 27:17

DISHONEST GAIN

Dishonest gain will never last, so why take the risk?   Proverbs 21:6

DISHONESTY

Don't place too much confidence in the man who boasts of being as honest as the day is long. Wait until you meet him at night.

DISOBEY

A mother was having trouble with her children on one of those indoor days when it was raining outside. Finally the harassed mother turned on them and said, "All right, do anything you please. NOW LET ME SEE YOU DISOBEY THAT!"

DISPUTES

A coin toss ends arguments and settles disputes between powerful opponents.   Proverbs 18:18

DISRESPECT

A woman who has made fun of her husband can love him no more.

DISTORT

First get your facts; and then you can distort them at your leisure.   Mark Twain

DISTRUST
Never trust a man who speaks well of everybody.

• • •

On one issue at least, men and women agree; they both distrust women.

• • •

Feel for others — in your pocket.
C. H. Spurgeon

DIVORCE
What a holler would ensue if people had to pay the minister as much to marry them as they have to pay a lawyer to get a divorce.

• • •

Dopey: "Why did the cow get a divorce?"
Dopier: "She got a bum steer."

• • •

One woman I know charged her husband with mental cruelty so severe it caused her to lose 30 pounds. "Divorce granted!" said the judge. "Oh, not yet," the woman pleaded. "First I want to lose another ten pounds."

DIVORCEE
A person who married for better or worse, but not for good.

DIZZY
Guy: Honey, your eyes make me dizzy.
Gal: Don't blame my eyes.

DOCTOR
The mistakes of doctors are hidden under the ground.

• • •

My doctor has an interesting approach to medicine. I opened my wallet and he said, "Ah!"

• • •

The best doctors in the world are Doctor Diet, Doctor Quiet, and Doctor Merryman.   Swift

• • •

Doctor: Shall I make an affidavit to the fact that he is dead?
Coroner: No, merely state that you treated him.

• • •

Patient: Doctor, do you think cranberries are healthy?
Doctor: I've never heard one complain.

• • •

My husband was very sick so we called Doctor Jones. My husband took his medicine and got worse. Then we called Doctor Vernon and my husband took his medicine and he got still worse. We thought he was going to die, so we called Doctor McKee and he was too busy, and finally my husband got well.

• • •

Dr. Hanson: So the operation on the man was just in the nick of time?
Dr. Poure: Yes, in another twenty-four hours he would have recovered.

• • •

"Doctor," said the pale-faced man to his physician, "I'm in an awful state! Whenever the phone rings, I almost jump out of my skin. The doorbell gives me the willies. If I see a stranger at the door, I start shaking. I'm even afraid to look at a newspaper.

What's come over me, anyway?''

The doctor patted him on the back sympathetically. ''There, there, old man. I know what you're going through. My teen-aged daughter just learned to drive, too.''

•   •   •

Patient: What would you charge to alter my nose?
Doctor: Five hundred dollars.
Patient: Anything cheaper?
Doctor: You can try walking into a telephone pole.

DOCTRINE

Any doctrine that will not bear investigation is not a fit tenant for the mind of an honest man.

DOGHOUSE

Mutt hut.

DO-IT-YOURSELF

A catalog ''do-it-yourself'' firm received the following letter from one of its customers.

''I built a birdhouse according to your stupid plans, and not only is it much too big, it keeps blowing out of the tree. Signed, Unhappy.''

The firm replied: ''Dear Unhappy: We're sorry about the mix-up. We accidentally sent you a sailboat blueprint. But if you think you are unhappy, you should read the letter from the guy who came in last in the Yacht Club regatta in a leaky birdhouse.''

DOLLAR

Jack of all trades.

DONKEY

Nothing passes between donkeys but kicks.

•   •   •

If your brother is a donkey, what are you?

DON'T

The best advice to give a man about to marry.

DOUBLE CHIN

She's got a couple of double chins. Every time she talks she broadcasts over short waves.

DOUBT

I will listen to any one's convictions, but pray keep your doubts to yourself. I have plenty of my own.

•   •   •

The best way to keep a husband is in doubt.

DOW JONES AVERAGE

...The Dow Jones average is roamin' numerals.

DRAUGHT

The first draught a man drinks ought to be for thirst, the second for nourishment, the third for pleasure, the fourth for madness.

DRESS

The body is the shell of the soul, and dress the husk of that shell; but the husk often tells what the kernel is.

•   •   •

If honor be your clothing, the suit will last a lifetime; but if clothing be your honor, it will soon be worn threadbare.

•   •   •

Dress changes the manners.

"Have you seen Sally's new dress?"

"No, what does it look like?"

"Well, in many places it's a lot like Sally."

DRINK

First the man takes a drink, then the drink takes a drink, then the drink takes the man.

• • •

A soft drink turneth away company.

DRINKING

Whose heart is filled with anguish and sorrow? Who is always fighting and quarreling? Who is the man with bloodshot eyes and many wounds? It is the one who spends long hours in the taverns, trying out new mixtures. Don't let the sparkle and the smooth taste of strong wine deceive you.

Proverbs 23:29-31

DRIPPING

A rebellious son is a calamity to his father, and a nagging wife annoys like constant dripping.

Proverbs 19:13

DRIVE

You can do more than strike while the iron is hot; you can make the iron hot by striking.

DRIVER

Only one American in two knows how to drive a car well, and she sits in the back seat.

DRIVING

Driving Instructor: "What would you do if you were going up an icy hill and the motor stalled and the brakes failed?"

Student: "I'd quickly adjust the rear view mirror."

DROWNED

Better go round than be drowned.

DRUM

Something to buy for your enemy's children.

• • •

If thine enemy wrong thee, buy each of his children a drum.

• • •

The first thing a child learns when he gets a drum is that he's never going to get another one.

DRUMMER

Boss to employee: "You may march to a different drummer, but I want the beat speeded up."

DRUNK

Let him who sins when drunk be punished when sober.

• • •

Don't ever give black coffee to a drunk. You'll end up with a wide-awake drunk on your hands.

DRYER

A sign on a dryer in a coin laundry reads: "This dryer is worthless." A sign on the next dryer reads: "This dryer is next to worthless."

DUCK

A chicken with snowshoes.

• • •

Chet: Never shoot a duck standing. You must shoot a duck on the wing.

Art: Can't I shoot him on the leg?

Chet: Yes, but you have to shoot him on the wing.

Art: How can I shoot him on the leg and shoot him on the wing?

Chet: Just remember to wing a duck on the wing and everything will be rosy.

Art: I know the game...Wing 'round the rosy.

•　•　•

Tim: How do you know you hit that duck?

Ken: I shot him in the foot and in the head at the same time.

Tim: How could you possibly hit him in the foot and head at the same time?

Ken: He was scratching his head.

DULL

The trouble with telling a good story is that it reminds the other fellow of a dull one.

DUMB

I didn't say he was dumb...I said he was twenty-years-old before he could wave good-bye.

DUTY

Best way to get rid of your duties is to discharge them.

•　•　•

I slept, and dreamed that life was Beauty;
I woke, and found that life was Duty.

•　•　•

For strength to bear is found in duty alone, and he is blest indeed who learns to make the joy of others cure his own heartache.

•　•　•

A duty dodged is like a debt unpaid; it is only deferred, and we must come back and settle the account at last.

•　•　•

Do something everyday that you don't want to do; this is the golden rule for acquiring the habit of doing your duty without pain.

Mark Twain

EARACHE

A lady complained of an earache so the doctor examined her and found a piece of string dangling from her right ear. The doctor began pulling it out, and the more he pulled, the more string came out. Suddenly the pulling became harder and he struggled with the string. To his amazement out fell a bouquet of roses.

The doctor exclaimed: "Good Gracious, where did this come from?"

"How should I know?" said the patient, "why don't you look at the card?"

EARTH

The pagans do not know God, and love only the earth. The Jews know the true God, and love only the earth. The Christians know the true God, and do not love the earth.　Blaise Pascal

EARTHQUAKE

Acre Shaker.

EATING

Eat, drink, and be merry, for tomorrow ye diet.

•　•　•

Doctors say that if you eat slowly you will eat less. You certainly will if you are a member of a large family.

•　•　•

He who does not mind his belly will hardly mind anything else.

Samuel Johnson

•   •   •

When it comes to eating, you can sometimes help yourself more by helping yourself less.

Richard Armour

•   •   •

We used to say, "What's cooking?" when we came home from work. Now it's "What's thawing?"

•   •   •

The proof of the pudding is in the eating.   Miguel de Cervantes

•   •   •

If you really want to lose weight, there are only three things you must give up: breakfast, lunch, and dinner.

EAVESDROPPING

Did you hear about the man who fell off the eaves of a building and was killed? That's what he deserves for eavesdropping.

ECHOES

There are many echoes in the world, but few voices.

ECONOMY

What this country needs is a good five-cent Nickel.

•   •   •

Rigid economy: A dead Scotsman.

•   •   •

Businessman, discussing the current economy: "The trouble is, everybody's buying on time but nobody's paying on time!"

ECONOMIST

An economist is a person who talks about something he doesn't understand and makes you believe you're ignorant.

ECSTASY

When all the children have grown up, married and moved away, most parents experience a strange new emotion. It's called ecstasy.

EDUCATION

Adult education is what goes on in a household containing teenage children!

•   •   •

If the cost of a college education continues to snowball for many more years, a person can make a profit by remaining ignorant.

•   •   •

I have never let my schooling interfere with my education.

Mark Twain

•   •   •

Education is too important to be left solely to the educators.

•   •   •

You can lead a boy to college, but you cannot make him think.

•   •   •

Education is a progressive discovery of our ignorance.

EFFICIENCY

It is more than probable that the average man could, with no injury to his health, increase his efficiency fifty percent.   Walter Scott

EFFORT

It is hard to fail, but it is worse never to have tried to succeed. In this life we get nothing save by effort.   Theodore Roosevelt

EGGS

Mother: Isn't it wonderful how little chicks get out of their shells?

Little Bufe: What beats me is how they get in.

EGO

The only thing that can keep on growing without nourishment.

EGOTIST

The egotist always hurts the one he loves — himself.

• • •

Egotist: A person of low taste, more interested in himself than in me.

• • •

From all bad comes a little good. An egotist never goes around talking about other people.

Guy: There are two men I really admire.

Gal: Who's the other one?

• • •

One nice thing about egotists: They don't talk about other people.

• • •

The mental cases most difficult to cure are the persons who are crazy about themselves.

EGRESS

It is said that Phineas T. Barnum, the famed circus magnate, hung a large sign over one of the exits of his museum, which read, "This way to the egress." Many people in the crowds, eager to see what an egress looked like, passed through the door and found themselves out on the street.

ELBOWS

Rubbing elbows with a man will reveal things about him you never suspected. The same is true of rubbing fenders.

ELEPHANTS

Why do elephants paint their toe nails purple?

So they can hide in grape vines.

Does it really work?

Have you ever seen an elephant in a grape vine?

• • •

Question: What would you do if an elephant sat in front of you in a movie?

Answer: Miss most of the picture.

• • •

Question: How do you sculpture an elephant?

Answer: You take a big block of marble and chip away anything that doesn't look like an elephant.

ELOQUENCE

Noise proves nothing. Often a hen who has merely laid an egg cackles as if she had laid an asteroid.   Mark Twain

• • •

True eloquence consists in saying all that is proper, and nothing more.

Francois de La Rochefoucauld

• • •

The finest eloquence is that which gets things done.

EMBARRASS

The young lady eyed her escort with great disapproval. "That's the fourth time you've gone back for more ice cream and cake, Albert," she said acidly. "Doesn't it embarrass you at all?"

"Why should it?" the hungry fellow shrugged. "I keep telling them I'm getting it for you."

EMBARRASSED

Preacher: Don't you get just a bit embarrassed to sing your own songs?

Singer: No. Don't some preachers preach their own sermons?

EMBARRASSING

Nothing is as embarrassing as watching your boss do something you assured him couldn't be done.

EMPLOYMENT

When you hire people that are smarter than you are, you prove you are smarter than they are.

EMPTY

He that is full of himself is empty.

● ● ●

There's nothing quite as empty as a stuffed shirt.

ENCORE

Comedian: "Look here, I do object to going on right after the monkey act."

Manager: "You're right. They may think it's an encore."

ENCOUNTER

Face to face clears many a case.

ENCOURAGEMENT

Kind words are like honey — enjoyable and healthful.

Proverbs 16:24

● ● ●

Anxious hearts are very heavy but a word of encouragement does wonders! Proverbs 12:25

● ● ●

Encouragement after censure is as the sun after a shower. Goethe

● ● ●

Some little word of encouragement may help a work as much as a great effort.

● ● ●

Johnny: "Lawrence is just bashful. Why don't you give him a little encouragement."

Bonnie: "Encouragement? He needs a cheering section!"

END

A big lion made a rush at me. I didn't want to kill him, so I took a stick and hit him on the tail...and that was the end of the lion.

ENDS

Why is it every time you start to make ends meet — somebody comes along and moves the ends?

ENDANGERED

One National Park ranger to another: "What do we do if we see an endangered animal eating an endangered plant?"

ENDURE

What cannot be cured
Must be endured.

ENEMY

The Bible tells us to love our neighbors and also to love our enemies, probably because they are generally the same people.

● ● ●

Observe your enemies, for they first find out your faults.

• • •

Everyone needs a warm personal enemy or two to keep him free from rust in the movable parts of his mind.

• • •

Love your enemies, for they tell you your faults.

• • •

President Lincoln was once taken to task for his attitude toward his enemies.

"Why do you try to make friends of them?" asked an associate.

"Am I not destroying my enemies," Lincoln gently replied, "when I make them my friends?"

• • •

If your enemy is hungry, give him food! If he is thirsty, give him something to drink! This will make him feel ashamed of himself, and God will reward you.

Proverbs 25:21-22

• • •

He overcomes a strong enemy who overcomes his own.

• • •

An open enemy is better than a false friend.

ENERGETIC
The energetic man and his bed are soon parted.

ENGLISH
High school principal speaking to a group of businessmen: "We require our boys to take English class for 4 years, we believe they should learn to speak a language other than their own."

ENJOYMENT
May we never let the things we can't have, or don't have, or shouldn't have, spoil our enjoyment of the things we do have and can have. As we value our happiness let us not forget it, for one of the greatest lessons in life is learning to be happy without the things we cannot or should not have.

ENTERTAIN
Be not forgetful to entertain strangers: for thereby some have entertained angels unawares. Bible

ENTHUSIASM
Enthusiasm comes from what I concentrate on.

EQUAL
Six feet of earth make all men equal.

ERASER
The best eraser in the world is a good night's sleep.

ERR
To err is human, but to admit it is not.

ERROR
Error always rides the back of truth.

• • •

To err is human, but when the eraser wears out ahead of the pencil, you're overdoing it.

• • •

The man who makes no mistakes does not usually make anything.

• • •

It takes less time to do a thing right than it does to explain why you did it wrong.

Henry Wadsworth Longfellow

ESCAPE

She was going to have an announcement party, but the engagement was broken...so she went ahead and called it a narrow-escape party.

• • •

The news media featured a convict's daring daylight escape from prison and his voluntary return and surrender later that evening. When reports asked him why he'd come back, he said, "The minute I sneaked home to see my wife, the first thing she said was, 'Where have you been? You escaped eight hours ago.'"

ESTATE

Lawyer: "Among other things, your uncle left you over five hundred clocks."

Heir: "Oh dear! It will take a long time to wind up his estate, won't it?"

ETIQUETTE

Learning to yawn with your mouth closed.

EVE

Eve was the first person who ate herself out of house and home.

• • •

Sunday School teacher: Class what do you know about Adam's wife, Eve?

Student: They named Christmas Eve for her.

• • •

Weary salesclerk: "Did you ever wonder how many fig leaves Eve tried on before she said, 'I'll take this one'?"

EVIL

To plan evil is as wrong as doing it.　　　　　Proverbs 24:8

• • •

It is a sin to believe evil of another, but it is seldom a mistake.

EXAGGERATE

Tim: You are beautiful. You are sweet, fine, wonderful. You are everything that's good.

Beverly: Oh, you flatterer, how you exaggerate.

Tim: Well, that's my story, and I'll stick to it.

EXAMPLE

Few things are harder to put up with than the annoyance of a good example.　　　Mark Twain

• • •

Example may be better than precept, but together they make a winning team.

• • •

He who lives well is the best preacher.　　　　Cervantes

• • •

Preach best in your own pulpit.

• • •

Preachers can talk but never teach.
Unless they practice what they preach.

• • •

Better an ounce of example than a pound of advice.

• • •

Few things are harder to put up with than the annoyance of a good example.　　　Mark Twain

• • •

Two things I've had in life, and

ample — good advice and bad example.

● ● ●

No man is completely worthless. He can always serve as a horrible example.

● ● ●

When small men cast big shadows, it means the sun is about to set.

EXCELLENT

Every good and excellent thing stands moment by moment on the razor's edge of danger and must be fought for.

EXCISE

Excise — how big she was before she took ''slim'' pills.

EXCITING

The backslider gets bored with himself; the godly man's life is exciting.   Proverbs 14:14

EXCUSE

An excuse is what a person says the reason is.

EXCUSES

He that is good for making excuses is seldom good for anything else.   Benjamin Franklin

EXECUTE

Execute every act of thy life as though it were thy last.

Marcus Aurelius

EXECUTIVE

An executive is a man who can make quick decisions that are right sometimes.

EXERCISE

A feeling that will go away if you just lie down for a little while.

EXPERIENCE

When I was a boy of fourteen, my father was so ignorant I could hardly stand to have the old man around. But when I got to be twenty-one, I was astonished at how much the old man had learned in seven years. Mark Twain

● ● ●

Experience is one thing you can't get for nothing. Oscar Wilde

● ● ●

The name that men give to their mistakes.

● ● ●

Men who leave home to set the world on fire, often come back for more matches.

● ● ●

Experience is the thing you have left when everything else is gone.

● ● ●

Ever notice that about the time you think you're to graduate from the school of experience, somebody thinks up a new course?

● ● ●

An employer interviewing an applicant remarked, ''You ask high wages for a man with no experience.''

''Well,'' he replied, ''it's so much harder to work when you don't know anything about it.''

● ● ●

Experience: The wonderful knowledge that enables you to recognize a mistake when you make it again.

EXPENSES

I never worry about meeting my expenses...I meet them whichever way I turn.

EXPERT

Question: What is the definition of an expert?

Answer: Someone called in at the last minute to share the blame.

• • •

A person who has no business of his own to wreck.

EXPLAIN

The man who takes time to explain his mistakes has little time left for anything else.

EXTERMINATOR

Exterminator's office: "We make mouse calls."

EXTREMES

Mistrust the man who finds everything good; the man who finds everything evil; and still more the man who is indifferent to everything.

EYES

Frances: Say, do your eyes bother you?

Walter: No...why?

Frances: Well, they bother me.

• • •

"Where'd you get those big eyes?"

"They came with the face."

• • •

Men were born with two eyes, but only one tongue, in order that they should see twice as much as they say.

• • •

He: What charming eyes you have.

She: I'm glad you like them. They were a birthday present.

FACE

"Your face would stop a clock."

"And yours would make one run!"

• • •

If your face is your fortune...you won't have to pay any income tax.

• • •

Something we would like to save, especially if we have lost our head.

FACE LIFT

"My uncle had his face lifted."

"How did they do it?"

"With a piece of rope around his neck."

FACTS

Get your facts first, and then you can distort them as much as you please.   Mark Twain

• • •

What a shame — yes, how stupid! — to decide before knowing the facts!   Proverbs 18:13

FAILURE

Ninety-nine percent of the failures come from people who have the habit of making excuses.

George Washington Carver

• • •

One who fails to keep on trying.

• • •

Never give a man up until he has failed at something he likes.

• • •

Failures are divided into two classes — those who thought and never did, and those who did and never thought.

• • •

Show me a thoroughly satisfied man and I will show you a failure.

Thomas A. Edison

•   •   •

Failure is only the opportunity to begin again, more intelligently.
Henry Ford

•   •   •

Half the failures in life arise from pulling in one's horse as he is leaping.

•   •   •

A man can fail many times, but he isn't a failure in life until he begins to blame somebody else.

Life is a grindstone, and whether it grinds a man down or polishes him up depends on the stuff he's made of.   Josh Billings

•   •   •

Lincoln: My great concern is not whether you have failed, but whether you are content with your failure.

FAIR

None but the brave can afford the fair.

FAIRNESS

We must be courteous to a man as we are to a picture, which we are willing to give the advantage of a good light.   Emerson

•   •   •

God is more pleased when we are just and fair then when we give Him gifts.   Proverbs 21:3

•   •   •

The Lord demands fairness in every business deal. He established this principle.   Proverbs 16:11

FAITH

Minister: "When in doubt, faith it."

•   •   •

If it weren't for faith, there would be no living in this world;

we couldn't even eat hash.
Josh Billings

•   •   •

Faith is the substance of things hoped for, the evidence of things not seen.   Hebrews 11:1, KJV

•   •   •

The just shall live by faith.
Romans 1:17, KJV

•   •   •

Faith goes up the stairs that love has made and looks out of the windows which hope has opened.
Charles Haddon Spurgeon

•   •   •

Fear knocked at the door. Faith answered. No one was there.

•   •   •

Faith without works is dead.
James 2:26, KJV

FAITHFUL

A faithful employee is as refreshing as a cool day in the hot summertime.   Proverbs 25:13

FAKE

Some clothes help to fake the man.

FALSE

Question: What do we call the last teeth to appear in the mouth?
Answer: False.

FALL

Don't fall in the fire to be saved from the smoke.

FALLING

Falling is easier than rising.

FAME

The ability to die at the right moment.

•   •   •

Fame is proof that people are gullible.   Ralph Waldo Emerson

FAMILIARITY
Though familiarity may not breed contempt, it takes off the edge of admiration.

FAMILY
The only thing missing in the American home.

●   ●   ●

The three stages of modern family life are matrimony, acrimony, and alimony.

●   ●   ●

A happy family is but an earlier heaven.

●   ●   ●

Nowadays, a family is a group of people who have keys to the same house.

●   ●   ●

The average American family consists of 4.1 persons. You have one guess as to who constitutes the .1 person.

FANATICISM
A fanatic is one who can't change his mind and won't change the subject.   Winston Churchill

FANS
What makes a baseball stadium cool?

Answer: The fans.

FAST
What one does while you try to get the waiter's attention.

●   ●   ●

He who lives too fast may live to fast.

FAT
He's so fat he can't tell where to bend over and where to sit down. So he has someone hit him with a board and if it knocks the wind out of him, he knows that side is his stomach.

●   ●   ●

Question: Why are you fat?
Answer: I'm not fat. I just retain flesh.

●   ●   ●

Question: How did you get so fat?
Answer: I became pregnant and I never gave birth. My baby decided to live in.

●   ●   ●

Question: You have such a pretty face, how come you let your figure go?
Answer: Because...as hard as I tried, I couldn't let my face go.

●   ●   ●

Question: Do you know it's not healthy to be so fat?
Answer: No...hum a few bars for me.

●   ●   ●

Question: How did you get so fat?
Answer: When I was a kid I got the mumps and it never cleared up.

●   ●   ●

Question: Are there any jobs for people as fat as yourself?
Answer: Yes. A stewardess on the Good Year Blimp.

●   ●   ●

Those ladies are so fat that it looks like the finals in the Miss Over-active Thyroid Contest.

FAT MAN

A man who always puts his best chin forward.

FATHER

Paternity is a career imposed on you without any inquiry into your fitness.

• • •

It is a wonderful heritage to have an honest father.   Proverbs 20:7

• • •

She: My father takes things apart to see why they don't go.

He: So what?

She: So you'd better go.

FAULTS

However blind a man may be, Another's faults he's sure to see.

• • •

A fault denied is twice committed.

FAVORS

O God, I beg two favors from you before I die: First, help me never to tell a lie. Second, give me neither poverty nor riches! Give me just enough to satisfy my needs! For if I grow rich, I may become content without God. And if I am too poor, I may steal, and thus insult God's holy name.

Proverbs 30:7-9

FEAR

Fear that man who fears not God.

• • •

Fear is the tax that conscience pays to guilt.

• • •

There's nothing I'm afraid of like scared people.   Robert Frost

FEEBLE

"Darling, will you love me when I'm old and feeble?"

"Yes, I do."

FEEL

"How do you feel?"

"I feel just like I look."

"That's too bad."

FENCE

The fence that makes good neighbors needs a gate to make good friends.

FENDER

The bent up side of your wife's car.

FIDELITY

Nothing is more noble, nothing more venerable than fidelity. Faithfulness and truth are the most sacred excellences and endowments of the human mind.   Cicero

FIFTY

"We've been married for fifty years."

"How does it feel?"

"Who feels after fifty years?"

FIGHTS

Fools start fights everywhere while wise men try to keep peace.

Proverbs 29:8

FILIBUSTER

The conversation of a bore.

FINANCE

Alexander Hamilton originated the put and take system in our national treasury: the taxpayers put it in, and the politicians take it out.   Will Rogers

• • •

One-third of the people in the United States promote, while the other two-thirds provide.

Will Rogers

FINANCE COMPANY

A conspiracy to extend a modest business...first established by Black Beard.

FINE

A fine is a tax for doing wrong. A tax is a fine for doing well.

● ● ●

Judge: And for the levity you have shown during your trial I shall give you an additional fine of $50. How does that suit you?

Prisoner: That's what I would call extra fine.

● ● ●

I'm fine, I'm fine
There's nothing whatever the matter with me
I'm just as healthy as I can be
I have arthritis in both of my knees
And when I talk, I talk with a wheeze.
My pulse is weak and my blood is thin
But I'm awfully well for the shape I'm in.
My teeth eventually will have to come out
And I can't hear a word unless you shout.
I'm overweight and I can't get thin
But I'm awfully well for the shape I'm in.
Arch supports I have for both my feet

Or I wouldn't be able to walk down the street
Sleep is denied me every night,
And every morning I'm really a sight.
My memory is bad and my head's a-spin
And I practically live on aspirin
But I'm awfully well for the shape I'm in.
The moral is, as this tale unfolds
That for you and me who are growing old,
It's better to say "I'm fine" with a grin
Than to let people know the shape we're in!"

FINISH

He who begins many things finishes few.

FINISHERS

The world has lots of starters but very few finishers.

FIRE

Sign on office bulletin board: "In case of fire don't panic. Simply flee the building with the same reckless abandon that occurs each day at quitting time."

FIRE INSURANCE

Bob: Does your uncle carry life insurance?

R.D.: No, he just carries fire insurance. He knows where he is going.

FIREPROOF

Fireproof: being related to the boss.

FISH

A large water creature that always seems to get away from a man.

* * *

A fish gains weight slowly, except the one that got away.

* * *

Fish and guests smell at three days old.

* * *

Brad: I've eaten beef all my life, and now I'm strong as an ox.

Rich: That's funny. I've eaten fish all my life and I can't swim a stroke.

FISHING

Why is it, whenever you go fishing, people will always ask, "Did you catch those fish?" What do they think—they jumped in the boat and surrendered?

* * *

Three-fourths of the Earth's surface is water and one fourth is land. It's obvious that the Good Lord intended that man should spend three times as much time fishing as plowing.

FLAGSTONE

Husband put in a flagstone walk from house to street. When he finished he called his wife to come look. "It is terrible, the colors don't match, the stones are crooked." Weary and disappointed he asked: "How is it for length?"

FLATTERY

The most dangerous of wild beasts is a slanderer; of tame ones, a flatterer.

* * *

If we did not flatter ourselves no one else could flatter us.

* * *

Many who would fight if offered a bribe, may be flattered into jumping off a house.

* * *

A flatterer: one who extremely exaggerates in his opinion of your qualities so that it may come nearer to your opinion of them.

* * *

To ask advice is in nine cases out of ten to tout for flattery.

* * *

Flattery is sweet food to those who can swallow it.

* * *

Flattery: phony express.

* * *

Fair words make me look to my purse.

* * *

Flattery is just a cheap lie.

* * *

Flattery is like cologne water, to be smelt of, not swallowed.

Abraham Lincoln

* * *

Avoid flatterers, for they are thieves in disguise.   William Penn

* * *

Flattery is from the teeth out. Sincere appreciation is from the heart out.   Dale Carnegie

* * *

Flattery is a trap; evil men are caught in it, but good men stay away and sing for joy.

Proverbs 29:5-6

* * *

Flattery is a form of hatred and wounds cruelly.   Proverbs 26:28

FLEA

Teacher: The man named Lot was warned to take his wife and flee out of the city, but his wife looked back and was turned to salt.

Student: "What happened to the flea?"

●   ●   ●

He that lies down with dogs will get up with fleas.

FLEE

The wicked flee when no one is chasing them! But the godly are bold as lions!   Proverbs 28:1

FLEECE

Sometimes we think the wicked fleece and no man pursueth.

FLEXIBILITY

Yale University: "The key to flexibility is indecision."

FLIRT

Sally: I wonder what's wrong with that tall blond guy over there. Just a minute ago he was getting awful friendly, and then all of a sudden he turned pale, walked away, and won't even look at me anymore.

Linda: Maybe he saw me come in. He's my husband.

FLIRTATION

...A flirtatious hen is a chicken coquette?

FLOORWALKERS

Parents of a newborn baby.

FLUID

Man to friend: "You might describe my financial situation as fluid. Which is a sort of nice way of saying I'm going down the drain."

FLU

Woman: "Do I have Asiatic Flu?"

Doctor: "No, you have Egyptian flu."

Woman: "What's that?"

Doctor: "You're going to become a mummy."

FLU SEASON

Hoarse and buggy days.

FOE

An open foe may prove a curse,
But a pretended friend is worse.

FOLLY

It is safer to meet a bear robbed of her cubs than a fool caught in his folly.   Proverbs 17:12

FOOD

The good man eats to live, while the evil man lives to eat.

Proverbs 13:25

●   ●   ●

Square meals make round people.

FOOL

After a big night on the town, one man was heard to say, "A fool and his money are some party."

●   ●   ●

In the mouth of a fool a proverb becomes as useless as a paralyzed leg.

●   ●   ●

No woman makes a fool out of a man...she merely directs the performance.

●   ●   ●

When two men quarrel there is at least one fool, and the man that interferes makes two.

●   ●   ●

He who would make a fool of himself will find many to help him.

He who is his own lawyer has a fool for a client.

It's a silly goose that comes to a fox's sermon.

We all know a fool when we see one — but not when we are one.

A fool gets into constant fights. His mouth is his undoing! His words endanger him.
                                    Proverbs 18:6-7

A fool and his money are soon parted.

The best way to convince a fool that he is wrong is to let him have his own way.   Josh Billings

No fools are so troublesome as those who have some wit.
                    Francois de La Rochfoucauld

FOOLED
Once bit twice shy.

FOOLISH
A foolish man may be known by six things: Anger without cause, speech without profit, change without progress, inquiry without object, putting trust in a stranger, and mistaking foes for friends.

FOOLS
Young men think old men are fools;
But old men know young men are fools.

Many that are wits in jest, are fools in earnest.

FOOT
Parents who are afraid to put their foot down usually have children who step on their toes.

Put your foot down where you mean to stand.

FOOTBALL
Seen on a car in New York City: "Talk to Your Wife Today — The Football Season Starts This Weekend."

The pastor of the Calvary Baptist Church in Tulsa calls this his "football theology":
Draft Choice: Selection of a pew near to or away from air-conditioning vents.
Bench Warmer: Inactive member.
In the Pocket: Where too many Christians keep their tithes.
Fumble: Lousy sermon.
Two-Minute Warning: Deacon in front row taking a peek at his watch in full view of the preacher.

"Uncle Robert, when does your football team play?" "Football team? What do you mean, my boy?" "Why, I heard father say that when you kicked off we'd be able to afford a big automobile."

FORGETFUL
"George is so forgetful," the sales manager complained to his secretary. "It's a wonder he can sell anything. I asked him to pick me up some sandwiches on his way back from lunch, and I'm not sure

he'll even remember to come back."

Just then the door flew open, and in bounced George. "You'll never guess what happened!" he shouted. "While I was at lunch, I met old man Brown, who hasn't bought anything from us for five years. Well, we got to talking and he gave me this half-million dollar order!"

"See," sighed the sales manager to his secretary. "I told you he'd forget the sandwiches."

FORGIVENESS

There is no revenge so complete as forgiveness.   Josh Billings

•   •   •

Always forgive your enemies — nothing annoys them so much.

Oscar Wilde

•   •   •

"I can forgive, but I cannot forget," is only another way of saying, "I will not forgive." Forgiveness ought to be like a cancelled note — torn in two, and burned up, so that it never can be shown against one.

Henry Ward Beecher

•   •   •

It is easier to forgive an enemy than a friend.

•   •   •

The weak can never forgive. Forgiveness is the attribute of the strong.   Mahatma Gandhi

•   •   •

To forget a wrong is the best revenge.

•   •   •

A small boy, repeating the Lord's Prayer one evening prayed:

"And forgive us our debts as we forgive those who are dead against us."

•   •   •

Every person should have a special cemetery lot in which to bury the faults of friends and loved ones.

•   •   •

It is easier for the generous to forgive, than for the offender to ask forgiveness.

•   •   •

Forgive us our debts, as we forgive our debtors.

Matthew 6:12, KJV

•   •   •

Forgiveness is the fragrance the violet sheds on the heel that has crushed it.   Mark Twain

•   •   •

Doing an injury puts you below your enemy; revenging one makes you but even with him; forgiving it sets you above him.

•   •   •

Forgiving the unrepentant is like drawing pictures on water.

FORK

If you drop a fork it's a sign company's coming...if a fork is missing it's a sign company's going.

FORTHRIGHT

"He's a very forthright character. He's right about a fourth of the time."

FRAGRANCE

It is always wise to stop wishing for things long enough to enjoy the fragrance of those now flowering.

FRANKNESS

It is an honor to receive a frank reply.　　　　Proverbs 24:26

●　　●　　●

In the end, people appreciate frankness more than flattery.
　　　　　　Proverbs 28:23

FRAU

Many a man lives by the sweat of his frau.

FREEDOM

I know but one freedom and that is the freedom of the mind.

●　　●　　●

Freedom is not free. Free men are not equal. Equal men are not free.

●　　●　　●

Man is really free only in God, the source of his freedom.

●　　●　　●

Those who expect to reap the blessings of freedom must, like men undergo the fatigues of supporting it.

●　　●　　●

Give your children too much freedom and you lose yours.

FREE SPEECH

Etta:　"Do you believe in free speech?"

Gretta:　"I certainly do."

Etta:　"Then may I make a long distance call on your telephone?"

●　　●　　●

Free speech isn't dead in Russia ...only the speakers.

●　　●　　●

It is by the goodness of God that in our country we have these three unspeakable precious things: Freedom of speech, freedom of con-science and the prudence never to practice either of them.
　　　　　　Mark Twain

FREETHINKER

One who is not married.

FRIEND

To a friend's house the road is never long.

●　　●　　●

What you eat yourself never gains you a friend.

●　　●　　●

A friend is:
a PUSH when you've STOPPED
a WORD when you're LONELY
a GUIDE when you're SEARCH-ING
a SMILE when you're SAD
a SONG when you're GLAD

●　　●　　●

To lose a friend is the greatest of all losses.

●　　●　　●

A friend is one who knows your faults yet loves you in spite of your virtues.

●　　●　　●

The best mirror is an old friend.

●　　●　　●

If you would win a man to your cause, first convince him that you are his sincere friend.　　　Lincoln

●　　●　　●

What is a Friend? I will tell you. It is a person with whom you dare to be yourself.

●　　●　　●

You can hardly make a friend in a year, but you can easily offend one in an hour.

●　　●　　●

Wounds from a friend are better than kisses from an enemy!

• • •

Who seeks a faultless friend rests friendless.

• • •

What is a friend: A single soul dwelling in two bodies.   Aristotle

• • •

Go often to the house of thy friend, for weeds choke up the unused path.   Shakespeare

• • •

He who puts a friend to public shame is as guilty as a murderer.

• • •

A friend is someone who knows all about you and likes you just the same.

• • •

A friend is one who knows you as you are, understands where you've been, accepts who you've become — and still, gently invites you to grow.

• • •

For many years a certain white whale and a tiny herring had been inseparable friends. Wherever the white whale roamed in search of food, the herring was sure to be swimming right along beside him.

One fine spring day the herring turned up off the coast of Norway without his companion. Naturally all the other fish were curious, and an octopus finally asked the herring what happened to the friend whale.

"How should I know?" the herring replied. "Am I my blubber's kipper?"

• • •

It's poor friendship that needs to be constantly bought.

• • •

Defend me from my friends; I can defend myself from my enemies.

• • •

Judge yourself by the friends you form.

• • •

Friends are like fiddle strings, they must not be screwed too tight.

• • •

True friends are greatest riches.

• • •

A man that hath friends must show himself friendly.   Bible

• • •

Choose your friends with care, that you may have choice friends.

• • •

A man dies as often as he loses his friends.

• • •

There are "friends" who pretend to be friends, but there is a friend who sticks closer than a brother.   Proverbs 18:24

FRIENDSHIP
Friendship is to be purchased only by friendship.

• • •

A man, sir, should keep his friendship in constant repair.

• • •

True friendship comes when silence between two people is comfortable.

• • •

Friendship is a plant that one must often water.

• • •

Friendship, like a bird, has two wings.

• • •

True friendship is a plant of slow growth.   Washington

• • •

Friendship doubles our joy and divides our grief.

• • •

If a man does not make new acquaintances as he advances through life, he will soon find himself left alone; one should keep his friendships in constant repair.   Samuel Johnson

FROG

In a frog-jumping contest in Calaveras County, California, the entry from the state of Kentucky was named Man-o-Wart.

FRUGAL

The man walked into the house panting and almost completely exhausted. "What happened, honey?" inquired his wife.

"It's a great new idea I have," he gasped. "I ran all the way home behind the bus and saved 50 cents."

"That wasn't very bright," replied his wife. "Why didn't you run behind a taxi and save $3.00?"

• • •

A rather frugal man asked the bank for a loan of one dollar and was told he would have to pay 7 percent interest at the end of the year. For security he offered $60,000 in U.S. bonds. The banker, forseeing a potential depositor, accepted the bonds and gave the man a dollar.

At the end of the year, he was back with a dollar and seven cents to clear up his debt and asked for the return of his bonds. Upon returning the bonds the banker asked, "I don't want to be inquisitive, but since you have all those bonds, why did you have to borrow a dollar?" "Well," said the tightfisted old gent, "I really didn't have to. But do you know of any other way I could get the use of a safety deposit box for seven cents a year?"

FRUSTRATION

Trying to find your glasses without your glasses.

FUNERAL

"Do you believe in life after death?" the boss asked one of his younger employees."

"Yes, sir."

"Well, then, that makes everything just fine," the boss went on. "About an hour after you left yesterday to go to your grandfather's funeral, he stopped in to see you."

• • •

A young minister was a bit late in arriving to perform a funeral. He forgot the name of the person who died and just before he went to the platform he leaned over to someone in the audience and asked, "Brother or sister?" "Cousin." came the reply.

FURROW

A plowman is known by his furrow.

FURY

Beware the fury of a patient man.

FUTURE

My interest is in the future

because I am going to spend the rest of my life there.

•   •   •

The best thing about the future is that it comes only one day at a time.

•   •   •

The trouble with our times is that the future is not what it used to be.

GAG

Something shoved down a person's throat whether he likes it or not.

GALAXIES

NASA reports galaxies are speeding away from earth at 90,000 miles a second. What do you suppose they know that we don't?

GAMBLING

He who gambles picks his own pocket.

•   •   •

An Ogden, Iowa, minister was matching coins with a member of his congregation for a cup of coffee. When asked if that didn't constitute gambling, the minister replied, "It is merely a scientific method of determining just who is going to commit an act of charity."

GAME WARDEN

"Are you the game warden?" asked a lady over the telephone.

"Yes, I am the game warden," was the reply.

"Oh, I am so glad," said the lady. "Will you please suggest some games for a little party I'm giving for my children?"

GARDEN

A good garden may have some weeds.

•   •   •

The more help I have in the garden, the more I like gardening.

GARDENER

A gardener is known by his garden.

GARGOYLE

A gargoyle is something you swallow when you have a sore throat.

GASOLINE

The way gas prices are today, anyone who gets less than 15 miles per gallon should have his hood examined.

•   •   •

I had a friend who drove his big new car into a filling station, saying, "Fill'er up." After a while, the filling station attendant suggested, "Better shut off your engine. You're gaining on me."

•   •   •

A boy and a girl were out driving one evening. They came to a quiet spot on a country lane, and the car stopped. "Out of gas," said the boy.

The girl opened her purse and pulled out a bottle.

"Wow!" said the boy. "A bottle...what is it?"

"Gasoline," said the girl.

GENIUS

Genius is only patience.

•   •   •

When a true genius appears in this world you may know him by the sign that the dunces are all in confederacy against him.

Jonathan Swift

• • •

Genius is one percent inspiration and ninety-nine percent perspiration.   Thomas A. Edison

GENERATION

Our generation never got a break. When we were young they taught us to respect our elders. Now that we're older, they tell us to listen to the youth of the country.

• • •

The older generation thought nothing of getting up at five every morning — and the younger generation doesn't think much of it either.

GENEROSITY

What seems to be generosity is often no more than disguised ambition, which overlooks a small interest in order to secure a great one.

• • •

If there be any truer measure of a man than by what he does, it must be by what he gives.

• • •

What I gave, I have; what I spent, I had; what I kept, I lost.

GENTLEMAN

A gentleman is one who never hurts anyone's feelings 'unintentionally.

• • •

Clowns are always best in their own company, but gentlemen are best everywhere.

• • •

Someone you don't know very well.

GENTLENESS

A gentle hand may lead an elephant with a hair.

• • •

Nothing is so strong as gentleness: nothing so gentle as real strength.   St. Francis de Sales

GEOMETRY

Geometry is easy as π

GERMINATE

Become a naturalized German.

GERMS

Husband: Don't put that money in your mouth . . .there's germs on it.

Wife: Don't be silly . . . even a germ can't live on the money you earn.

GET EVEN

The best way to get even is to forget.

GETTING STARTED

He has half the deed done, who has made a beginning.

GHOST

Ghost writers: Spooksmen.

GIVE

The hardest thing to give is in.

• • •

It is better to give than to lend, and it costs about the same.

• • •

However much a man gives, there is more that he withholds.

GIVING

What you save, you leave behind; what you spend, you have

for awhile, but what you give away, you take with you.

•   •   •

Giving gifts from the heart never makes a poor man.   Phillips

•   •   •

The poorest can give as much as the richest if he will give all he can.

•   •   •

Gifts should be handed, not thrown.

•   •   •

He who gives when he is asked has waited too long.

•   •   •

Too often a cheerful giver is cheerful only because he's got away with giving as little as possible.

•   •   •

When it comes to giving, some people stop at nothing.

•   •   •

One who doesn't give the gift he promised is like a cloud blowing over a desert without dropping any rain.   Proverbs 25:14

•   •   •

When you help the poor you are lending to the Lord — and He pays wonderful interest on your loan!
                    Proverbs 19:17

•   •   •

It is possible to give away and become richer! It is also possible to hold on too tightly and lose everything. Yes, the liberal man shall be rich! By watering others, he waters himself.
                    Proverbs 11:24-25

•   •   •

Pastor: "You claim you can't donate be- cause you owe everyone. Don't you owe the Lord something?"

Parishioner: "Yes, but He isn't pushing me like the rest are."

•   •   •

"Give until it hurts."
"Here's a quarter."
"You can't stand much pain."

GIFT
Another name for trade.

GIRLS
I never expected to see the day when girls would get sunburned in the places they do now. Will Rogers

•   •   •

A girl is innocence playing in the mud, beauty standing on its head, and motherhood dragging a doll by the foot.

•   •   •

Some girls play hard to get until they become hard to take.

•   •   •

When a boy breaks a date, he usually has to. When a girl breaks a date, she usually has two.

•   •   •

Some girls don't think about boys all the time. They just think about them when they think.

GLASSES
Walter: I had trouble with my eyes...I saw spots in front of my eyes.
Frances: Do your glasses help?
Walter: Yes, now I can see the spots much better.

GLASS EYE
Christy: That lady has a glass eye.
Lisa: How did you find that out?

Christy: Well, it just came out in the conversation.

GLEAM
Did you hear about the man with the gleam in his eye? Somebody bumped him while he was brushing his teeth.

GLOOMY
When a man is gloomy, everything seems to go wrong: when he is cheerful, everything seems right!

Proverbs 15:15

GLUTTON
One who digs his grave with his teeth.

GNU
Mama Gnu was waiting for Papa Gnu as he came home for dinner one evening. "Our little boy was very bad today," she declared. "I want you to punish him."

"Oh no," said Papa Gnu. "I won't punish him. You'll have to learn to paddle your own gnu.

GOBLET
A goblet is a male turkey.

GOD
I fear God, and next to God I chiefly fear him who fears Him not.

•   •   •

He who leaves God out of his reckoning does not know how to count.

•   •   •

Nobody talks so constantly about God as those who insist that there is no God.

•   •   •

He who does not believe that God is above all is either a fool or has no experience of life.

Caecilius Statius

•   •   •

Sunday School Teacher: Why do you believe in God?

Small student: I guess it just runs in our family.

GODLINESS
Godly men are growing a tree that bears life-giving fruit, and all who win souls are wise.

Proverbs 11:30

GO-GETTER
One who gets in behind you in a revolving door and comes out ahead of you.

•   •   •

Question: What do they call a man who runs out of gas three miles from a station?

Answer: A go-getter.

GOING STEADY
In the old days a boy would give his girl his class ring when they were going steady, now he lets her use his hair curlers.

GOLF
Man to friend: "After three sets of clubs and ten years of lessons, I'm finally getting some fun out of golf. I quit."

•   •   •

Wife to husband at front door carrying golf clubs: "You don't have to go all the way to the golf course for a hole in one. There's one in the roof, one in the screen door, and one in the . . ."

•   •   •

Golf is a lot of walking, broken up by disappointment and bad arithmetic.

•   •   •

By the time you're old enough to afford losing golf balls, you're not hitting them that far.

•   •   •

Wife at 2 a.m. "Where have you been?"
Husband: "Playing golf."
Wife: "After dark?"
Husband: "Yes, we were using night clubs."

•   •   •

Many a man who doesn't play golf can't give it up.

GOLF CART
On golf cart: "No hitch-hackers."

GOLF CLUB
Another name for a shovel.

GOLD
One trouble is that nations are not only off the gold standard, but the golden rule standard.

•   •   •

Gold goes in at any gate except heaven's.

GOOD-BY
Something that money says.

GOODNESS
Be good and you will be lonesome.   Mark Twain

GOOD NEWS
Good news from far away is like cold water to the thirsty.

GOOD OLD DAYS
Too many people keep looking forward to the good old days.

•   •   •

1880..."I walked 14 miles through snow and rain to go to school."
1915..."I had to walk five miles every day."
1936..."It was eleven blocks to the bus stop every morning."
1950..."I had to buy gasoline for my own car."
1966..."When I drove to school as a boy, we didn't have power brakes, power steering, or power windows."

GOSSIP
The gossip's mouth costs her nothing, for she never pens it but at another's expense.   Franklin

•   •   •

Meddle not with dirt; some of it will stick to your fingers.

•   •   •

Gossip: Knife of the party.

•   •   •

Who gossips to you will gossip of you.

•   •   •

Not everyone repeats gossip. Some improve it.

•   •   •

If nobody listened,
To whom would gossips talk?

•   •   •

If you would like to be talked about, leave the party before the rest do.

•   •   •

Unimpeachable source: The person who started the rumor originally.

•   •   •

When gossips meet, the devil goes to dinner.

•   •   •

Gossips are the spies of life.

Of every ten persons who talk about you, nine will say something bad, and the tenth will say something good in a bad way.

The only time people dislike gossip is when you gossip about them.   Will Rogers

None are so fond of secrets as those who do not mean to keep them.

Fire goes out for lack of fuel, and tensions disappear when gossip stops.   Proverbs 26:20

An evil man sows strife; gossip separates the best of friends.
                    Proverbs 16:28

A gossip goes around spreading rumors, while a trustworthy man tries to quiet them. Proverbs 11:13

Don't tell your secrets to a gossip unless you want them broadcast to the world.   Proverbs 20:19

Gossip is a dainty morsel eaten with great relish.   Proverbs 26:22

Question: What do they call someone who puts who and who together and gets wow!
Answer: A gossip.

She has ears like steam shovels... they're always picking up dirt.

Gossip that comes over the grapevine is usually sour.

"Now listen, did you tell Sara that what you said was in strict confidence?"

"Oh no; I didn't want her to think it was important enough to repeat."

GOVERNMENT

A large plant that needs more pruning and less grafting.

Most people would be glad to tend their own business if the government would give it back.

We all work for the government but the politician is wise. He gets paid for it.

Measuring big government by the magnitude of a billion:

1 billion seconds ago — the bombing of Pearl Harbor.

1 billion minutes ago — Christ was living on earth.

1 billion hours ago — man had not yet appeared on earth, but

1 billion dollars ago—that was only yesterday.

It's becoming more and more difficult to support the government in the style to which it has become accustomed.

GRACE

One blistering hot day when they had guests for dinner, the mother asked 4-year-old Johnny to say grace. "But I don't know what to say," the boy explained.

"Oh, just say what you hear me say," the mother replied.

Obediently, the boy bowed his

head and murmured, "Oh, Lord, why did I invite these people here on a hot day like this."

• • •

The following mealtime prayer was overheard: "Some people have food but no appetite; others have appetite, but no food. I have both. The Lord be praised."

GRADE

Little Charlie came home with an O on his homework. Naturally, his mother wanted to know why he got an O. "Charlie," she said, "Why is there an O on this paper?"

"That's no O," said Charlie. "The teacher ran out of stars and gave me a moon!"

GRAFFITI

Wit-and-run literature.

GRANDCHILDREN

"Have I told you about my grandchildren?"

"No, and I thank you very much."

GRANDFATHER

"When my grandfather died he left me $10,000."

"That's nothing. When my grandfather died he left the earth."

GRAPE

Question: What's purple and 5000 miles long?
Answer: The Grape Wall of China.

GRATITUDE

If you pick up a starving dog and make him prosperous, he will not bite you. This is the principal difference between a dog and a man.   Mark Twain

GRAVE

A grave, wherever found, preaches a short and pithy sermon to the soul.   Nathaniel Hawthorne

• • •

The only difference between a rut and a grave is their dimensions.
                        Ellen Glasgow

GREAT

The great man is he who does not lose his child's heart.

GREATNESS

In admiring greatness we rise to its level.

GREASE

I hate to be a kicker, I always long for peace,

But the wheel that does the squeaking is the one that gets the grease.   Josh Billings

GREMLIN

An elf-made man.

GRIEVES

He grieves more than is necessary who grieves before it is necessary.   Seneca

GRIPING

Man who beef too much find himself in stew.

GROAN

The result of reading this joke book.

GROW

You grow up the day you have your first real laugh — at yourself.
                        Ethel Barrymore

GROWLS

Ken: Does your father have a den?
Melba: He doesn't need one. He just growls all over the house.

GRUDGE
No matter how much you nurse a grudge it won't get better.

GROUP THERAPY
Did you hear about those new group-therapy luncheons . . .they are called "Wining and Dining."

GUEST
A constant guest is never welcome.

•   •   •

Fish and guests smell at three days old.

•   •   •

Unbidden guests are welcomest when they are gone.

GUIDANCE
Teach a child to choose the right path, and when he is older he will remain upon it.

GUIDE
A fishing party was hopelessly lost in the deep woods. "I thought you were the best guide in Minnesota," said one man.
"I am," replied the guide, "but I think we're in Canada now."

GUILT
Every guilty person is his own hangman.   Seneca

•   •   •

From the body of one guilty deed a thousand ghostly fears and haunting thoughts proceed.
                    William Wordsworth

•   •   •

He confesses his guilt who evades a trial.

GUILTY
The guilty catch themselves.

GURU
Guru to guest: "There are several meanings of life — a $50 meaning, a $100 meaning and one for $500."

GUTTER
Then there was the sanitation worker who got fired because he couldn't keep his mind in the gutter.

•   •   •

"He's a great detective...he's always got his ear to the ground. In fact, he's always in the gutter."

HABIT
Habit is a cable; we weave a thread of it every day, and at last we cannot break it.   Horace Mann

•   •   •

Nothing so needs reforming as other people's habits. Mark Twain

•   •   •

Habit, if not resisted, soon becomes necessity.   St. Augustine

•   •   •

The unfortunate thing about this world is that the good habits are much easier to give up than the bad ones.
                    W. Somerset Maugham

•   •   •

Sow an act and you reap a habit.
Sow a habit and you reap a character.
Sow a character and you reap a destiny.   Charles Reade

•   •   •

Habit is habit and not to be flung out of the window by any man, but coaxed downstairs a step at a time.   Mark Twain

•   •   •

Good habits result from resisting temptation.

•   •   •

A habit is a shirt made of iron.

● ● ●

A nail is driven out by another nail; habit is overcome by habit.

● ● ●

Habits are cobwebs first; cables at last.

HAIRDO

We're constantly amazed at these young things with their fancy hairdos and skin tight pants. And the girls are even worse.

HALF

Half the world knows how the other half ought to live.

HALF-TRUTH

Beware of a half-truth; it may be the wrong half.

HALFWAY

Doing things by halves is worthless. It may be the other half that counts.

HALITOSIS

Better than no breath at all.

HALLS OF CONGRESS

Lobbyrinth.

HALOS

Bent Halos Repaired Here.

HAMLET

A hamlet is an English dish consisting of ham and eggs cooked together.

HANDS

Many hands make light work: this is clear.

Many hands make slight work: this I fear.

HANGED

The applicant for life insurance was finding it difficult to fill out the application. The salesman asked what the trouble was and the man said that he couldn't answer the question about the cause of death of his father.

The salesman wanted to know why. After some embarrassment the client explained that his father had been hanged.

The salesman pondered for a moment. "Just write: 'Father was taking part in a public function when the platform gave way.'"

HANGERS

Oh, what a tangled web we weave, when first we drop a bunch of clothes hangers.

HAPPINESS

Happiness is the art of making a bouquet of those flowers within reach.

● ● ●

Happiness is like perfume: spray it on others and you are bound to get some on yourself.

● ● ●

All happy families resemble one another; every unhappy family is unhappy in its own fashion. Tolstoi

● ● ●

It is no sillier for the rich to think the poor are happy than for the poor to think the rich are.

● ● ●

Happiness is no laughing matter.

● ● ●

It is pretty hard to tell what does bring happiness; poverty and wealth have both failed.

● ● ●

Pleasant sights and good reports give happiness and health.

Proverbs 15:30

HAPPY
Ken: For 18 long years my girl and I were deliriously happy.

Bob: Then what happened?

Ken: We met.

HAPPY-GO-LUCKY
Being happy-go-lucky around a person whose heart is heavy is as bad as stealing his jacket in cold weather, or rubbing salt in his wounds.   Proverbs 25:20

HARD
Hard hits make hard hearts.

HARDWORK
Work hard and become a leader; be lazy and never succeed.
                                Proverbs 12:24

•   •   •

Hard work means prosperity; only a fool idles away his time.
                                Proverbs 12:11

HARP
A nude piano.

HASTE
He who pours water hastily into a bottle spills more than he saves.

•   •   •

Hasty climbers have sudden falls.

•   •   •

Make haste slowly.

•   •   •

Though I am always in haste, I am never in a hurry.   John Wesley

•   •   •

Marry in haste, and you'll never have any leisure to repent in.

•   •   •

Do not be in a desperate hurry, or you will get into trouble, or at least fail in your endeavors. The Chinese say that "a hasty man drinks his tea with a form."

HAT
His name was Seven-and-a-quarter. They had picked his name out of a hat.

HATCHET
What a hen does to an egg.

HATE
To hate fatigues.

•   •   •

I shall never permit myself to stoop so low as to hate any man.
                        Booker T. Washington

•   •   •

A man with hate in his heart may sound pleasant enough, but don't believe him; for he is cursing you in his heart. Though he pretends to be so kind, his hatred will finally come to light for all to see.   Proverbs 26:24-26

HAYSTACK
City Slicker: What kind of a house is that?

Farmer: That's not a house, that's a haystack.

City Slicker: You can't fool me, hay doesn't grow in a lump like that.

HEADWAITER
A tyrant without ears or eyes dressed in a tuxedo.

HEALTH
Better a healthy peasant than a sickly king.

•   •   •

There's a lot of people in this world who spend so much time watching their health that they haven't time to enjoy it.

Josh Billings

HEAR

Don't see all you see, and don't hear all you hear.

HEARING AID

A rather frugal gentleman was becoming increasingly hard of hearing, but decided a hearing aid was too expensive so he wrapped an ordinary piece of wire around his ear. "Do you hear better now with that wire around your ear?" asked a friend.

"Not a bit," came the reply, "but everybody talks louder."

● ● ●

Hearing-aid center: "Let us give you some sound advice."

HEART

Two things are bad for the heart — running up stairs and running down people.

● ● ●

Brave hearts are tender hearts.

● ● ●

The great man is he who does not lose his child's heart.

HEAVEN

As much of heaven is visible as we have eyes to see.

● ● ●

I don't like to commit myself about heaven and hell — you see, I have friends in both places.

Mark Twain

HELL

The road to Hell is paved with good intentions.   Karl Marx

● ● ●

The wicked work harder to reach hell than the righteous to reach heaven.   Josh Billings

● ● ●

If there is no hell, a good many preachers are obtaining money under false pretenses.

William A. Sunday

● ● ●

Hell is truth seen too late — duty neglected in its season.

● ● ●

A motorist was picked up unconscious after a smash, and was being carried to a nearby filling station. Upon opening his eyes en route, he began to kick and struggle desperately to get away. Afterwards he explained that the first thing he saw was a "Shell" sign, and somebody was standing in front of the "S"!

● ● ●

The trouble about dying and going below is, when you get mad at your friends, where do you tell them to go.

● ● ●

"There will be weeping, wailing and gnashing of teeth among the wicked who pass on to the next world."

"What about those who haven't any teeth?"

"Teeth will be provided."

HELP

God helps those who cannot help themselves.

● ● ●

Give me the ready hand rather than the ready tongue.

Guseppi Garibaldi

HEN

If you would have a hen lay, you must bear with her cackling.

HEREDITY

Nearly every man is a firm believer in heredity until his son makes a fool of himself.

HESITATE

She who hesitates is lost; so is the man who doesn't.

HEROISM

The main thing about being a hero is to know when to die.

Will Rogers

HICCUPS

We've just heard about a glass blower who was suddenly overcome by hiccups. He turned out a thousand percolator caps before help came.

HIDE

God hides things by putting them near us.

HIGH HORSE

Nothing is as hard to do gracefully as getting down off your high horse.

HIPPIE

A hippie lived in a room with just one chair and a cot for furniture. One night a friend dropped in, and spying two magazines lying in the middle of the floor asked, "Whadja do, man, hire an interior decorator?"

• • •

A fellow noticed a flower-bedecked, flowing-haired hippie walking down the street with a cigar box under his arm so he stopped him and asked, "How much are your cigars?"

"I'm not selling cigars," came the answer. "I'm moving."

HIPPOPOTAMUS

The teacher took her class to the zoo. When they passed the lion's cage, she asked "What's the plural of lion?"

One of the boys answered, "lions."

"What's the plural of sheep?" she asked.

One of the girls answered, "sheep."

"Right," said the teacher. A little farther along they came upon a hippopotamus.

"What's the plural of hippopotamus?" the teacher asked little Johnny.

Johnny shuddered. "Who would want two of **those**?"

HISTORY

History is what enables each nation to use the other fellow's past record as an alibi.

HITLER

A very naziating man.

• • •

Adolph Hitler was an avid believer in astrology and consulted with his special astrologist before making any decisions.

One day in consulting with him, Hitler asked, "On what day will I die?"

"You will die on a Jewish holiday," replied the astrologist.

"How can you be so sure of that?" asked Hitler.

"Any day you die will be a Jewish holiday," replied the astrologist.

HOBBY

Voluntary work.

HOME

Home is where you can be silent and still be heard...where you can ask and find out who you are...where people laugh with you about yourself...where sorrow is divided and joy multiplied...where we share and love and grow.

• • •

The worst feeling in the world is the homesickness that comes over a man occasionally when he is at home.

• • •

A hundred men may make an encampment, but it takes a woman to make a home.

• • •

There's no place like home.

• • •

The home can be the strongest ally of the Sunday School or its greatest enemy, depending on the parents.

• • •

Nothing makes you feel that your home is your castle more than getting an estimate to have it painted.

HOMESICK

"Honest, weren't you ever homesick?"

"Not me, I never stay there long enough."

HOMICIDE

Homicide is when a man kills himself in his own home.

HONESTY

Honesty pays, but it don't seem to pay enough to suit some people.

• • •

A little, gained honestly, is better than great wealth gotten by dishonest means.   Proverbs 16:8

• • •

It pays to be honest, but it's slow pay.

• • •

Lies will get any man into trouble, but honesty is its own defense.   Proverbs 12:13

HONEY

Do you like honey? Don't eat too much of it, or it will make you sick!   Proverbs 25:16

HONOR

The louder he talked of his honor, the faster we counted our spoons.   Ralph Waldo Emerson

HONORS

Just as it is harmful to eat too much honey, so also it is bad for men to think about all the honors they deserve!   Proverbs 25:27

HOPE

Those who hope for no other life are dead even in this.
     Johann Wolfgang von Goethe

HORN

The horn of plenty is the one the guy behind you has on his car.

• • •

Get someone else to blow your horn and the sound will carry twice as far.   Will Rogers

HORSE

He that can travel well afoot keeps a good horse.   Franklin

HORSERADISH

A minister who was very fond of pure, hot horseradish always kept a bottle of it on his dining room table. He offered some to a guest, who took a big bite.

When the guest finally was able

to speak: "I've heard many preach hellfire, but you are the first one I've met who passed out a sample of it."

HORSE SENSE

Question: What is another name for stable thinking.

Answer: Horse sense.

HORSE STEALING

Teacher: Name one of the benefits of the automotive age.

Student: It has practically stopped horse stealing.

HOUSE

Every girl can keep house better than her mother till she tries.

• • •

The crown of the house is Godliness. The beauty of the house is order. The glory of the house is hospitality. The blessing of the house is love.

• • •

When are houses like books?
When they have stories in them.

HOUSEHOLD

The only males who boss the household are under three years old.

HOSPITALITY

Don't open your door and darken your countenance.

• • •

Behave towards everyone as if receiving a great guest.

HOSTILITY

It is better to live in a corner of an attic than in a beautiful home with a cranky, quarrelsome woman.
Proverbs 25:24

• • •

Said one man to another: "You didn't laugh at Smith's joke. I thought it was quite a good one."

"It was a good one," replied the other, "but I can't stand Smith. I'll laugh when I get home."

HOT DOG

The Hot Dog is the noblest of all dogs because it feeds the hand that bites it.

HOTEL

You asked me how I liked this hotel. Well, it's so run-down that when you leave the key in the door, you cut off all the air.

HOT-HEADED

Hot-heads make their brains bubble over.

• • •

Don't be hot-headed and rush to court! You may start something you can't finish and go down before your neighbor in shameful defeat. So discuss the matter with him privately. Don't tell anyone else, lest he accuse you of slander and you can't withdraw what you said.
Proverbs 25:8-10

HOT-TEMPERED

A hot-tempered man starts fights and gets into all kinds of trouble.
Proverbs 29:22

HUGGING

Buck: Did you ever wonder why there are so many more auto wrecks than railway accidents?

Bufe: Did you ever hear of the fireman hugging the engineer?

HUMAN NATURE
It is easier to love humanity as a whole than to love one's neighbor.

• • •

Some of us are like wheelbarrows — only useful when pushed, and very easily upset.

HUMBLE
Better poor and humble than proud and rich.   Proverbs 16:19

HUMOR
A sense of humor is the pole that adds balance to our steps as we walk the tightrope of life.

• • •

Never risk a joke with a man who is unable to comprehend it.

• • •

Good humor is the health of the soul; sadness its poison.

• • •

I can usually judge a fellow by what he laughs at.

• • •

If I had no sense of humor, I would long ago have committed suicide.   Mahatma Gandhi

• • •

A man isn't poor if he can still laugh.

• • •

If I studied all my life, I couldn't think up half the number of funny things passed in one session of Congress.   Will Rogers

• • •

Everything is funny as long as it is happening to somebody else.
        Will Rogers

• • •

Whenever you find humor, you find pathos close by his side.

• • •

There are very few good judges of humor, and they don't agree.
        Josh Billings

HUMORIST
Will Rogers once said it's no big deal being a humorist when you have the whole government working for you.

• • •

A person who originates old jokes.

HUNGER
A hungry man is not a free man.
        Adlai E. Stevenson

• • •

An empty stomach is not a good political advisor.   Albert Einstein

• • •

Hunger is good — if it makes you work to satisfy it!
        Proverbs 16:26

HUSBAND
A man of few words.

• • •

An archaeologist is the best husband any woman can have: the older she gets, the more interested he is in her.   Agatha Christie

• • •

One good husband is worth two good wives; for the scarcer things are, the more they are valued.

HYPOCHONDRIAC
One who enjoys poor health.

HYPOCRISY
A hypocrite is a fellow who isn't himself on Sundays.

HYPOCRITE
Hypocrite: the man who murdered both his parents...pleaded for mercy on the grounds that he was an orphan.   Abraham Lincoln

A man who sets good examples when he has an audience.

ICICLE

A hunter was out in the forest. It was late in the day and getting colder. A bear appeared. The hunter grabbed his gun — there was no ammunition left! He wiped the sweat off his brow and put it in the gun — it shot out as an icicle and pierced the head of the bear and the bear died of water on the brain!

IDEAL

An ideal wife is any woman who has an ideal husband.

IDEAS

Many ideas grow better when transplanted into another mind than in the one where they sprung up.   Oliver Wendell Holmes

Ideas are very much like children — our own are very wonderful.

"I've got an idea."
"Be kind to it. It's a long way from home."

IDENTITY CRISIS

A lot of people don't realize they have an identity crisis until they try to cash a check in a strange town.

IDIOT

My wife thinks she's changed. She's always talking about what an idiot she used to be.

"When I was a child I used to bite my fingernails; and the doctor told me if I didn't quit it I'd grow up to be an idiot."
"And you couldn't stop, huh?"

Our town was too small to have a village idiot so we all took turns.

IDLENESS

An idle brain is the devil's workshop.

Laziness grows on people; it begins in cobwebs and ends in iron chains.

Prolonged idleness paralyzes initiative.

Idle people are dead people that you can't bury.

Idle bodies are generally busy-bodies. .

An idle man is the devil's play-fellow.

Idle hands are the devil's workshop; idle lips are his mouthpiece.
          Proverbs 16 : 27

IDOLATRY

The idol is the measure of the worshipper.   James Russell Lowell

IGLOO

Domicicle.

IGNORAMUS

It's difficult to define the word, "ignoramus," unless one has studied himself pretty carefully.

IGNORANCE

He knows so little and knows it so fluently.   Ellen Glasgow

Everybody is ignorant, only on different subjects.　　Will Rogers

• • •

Occasionally you meet a person whose only job is spreading ignorance.

• • •

You can say one thing for ignorance — it certainly causes a lot of interesting arguments.

• • •

Where there is ignorance of God, the people run wild; but what a wonderful thing it is for a nation to know and keep His laws!　　Proverbs 29:18

• • •

"Do I understand the speaker thanks God for his ignorance?"

"Yes, you can put it that way if you wish."

"All I can say then, is that he has a great deal to thank God for."

IMAGE

Mother: The baby is the image of his father.

Neighbor: What do you care, so long as he is healthy.

IMITATION

Imitation is the sincerest flattery.

• • •

"I'm rather good at imitations. I can imitate almost any bird you can name."

"How about a homing pigeon."

IMPASSABLE

A wet football.

IMPATIENCE

He who is impatient waits twice.

IMPERFECTIONS

'Tis a mark of great perfection to bear with the imperfections of others.

IMPOSSIBLE

Professor: Nothing is impossible. Nothing that mind of man can conceive is impossible.

Student: Did you ever try to strike a match on a marshmallow?

IMPOSSIBILITY

The difficult is that which can be done immediately; the impossible that which takes a little longer.

IMPRESS

Father to teenage son: "Mind if I use the car myself tonight? I'm taking your mother out and I want to impress her."

IMPROVE

Of all the awkward people in your house there is only one whom you can improve very much.

• • •

People seldom improve when they have no other model but themselves to copy after.

INCOME

Our incomes are like our shoes: if too small, they pinch, if too large, we stumble.

INCOME TAX

An income tax return is like a girdle. If you put the wrong figure in it, you're apt to get pinched.

INDECISION

Indecision: under the whether.

• • •

Once I make up my mind, I'm full of indecision.

●   ●   ●

Graffito on the wall at the London Observer: "The editor's indecisions are final."

●   ●

Indecision is the graveyard of good intentions.

INDEPENDENCE

It is not the greatness of a man's means that makes him independent, so much as the smallness of his wants.

INDEPENDENT

Rod: Are you independent on your new job?

Ron: I should say so! I go to work anytime I want to before 7 and quit any time I get ready after 5 o'clock.

INDIAN

Clerk: This jug was made by a real Indian.

Elmer: But it says here it's made in Cleveland, Ohio.

Clerk: Well, didn't you ever hear of the Cleveland Indians?

INDIGNANT

The young matron was breezing along in the left-hand lane when suddenly and without warning, she made a sharp right turn and almost slammed into another car.

"For Pete's sake, lady, why didn't you signal?" yelled the other driver.

"Don't be ridiculous," came the indignant reply, "I always turn here."

INDISTINCT

Question: Where do people put dirty dishes?

Answer: Indistinct.

INDUSTRY

A man who gives his children habits of industry provides for them better than by giving them a fortune.

INFLATION

Two can still live as cheaply as one...if one doesn't show up.

●   ●   ●

Inflation is when the buck doesn't stop anywhere.

●   ●   ●

Inflation marches on, making it possible for people in all walks of life to live in more expensive neighborhoods without ever moving.

●   ●   ●

I have it all figured out. If I continue saving at the present rate, I'll retire owing $50,000.

●   ●   ●

The way prices keep going up, the next thing we know they'll have the bargain basement on the third floor.

●   ●   ●

One good thing about inflation is that it's practically impossible for a youngster to get sick on a 5-cent candy bar.

INFERIORITY

Then there was the teen whose spirit was so low that he told his buddy, "The only way I can feel superior is by seeing that my inferiority complex is bigger than any one else's."

●   ●   ●

No one can make you feel inferior without your consent.

Eleanor Roosevelt

•   •   •

We must interpret a bad temper as a sign of inferiority. Alfred Adler

•   •   •

No man likes to have his intelligence or good faith questioned, especially if he has doubts about it himself.

Henry Brooks Adams

INFERIORS

A person who talks about his inferiors hasn't any.

•   •   •

One of the most considerable advantages the great have over their inferiors is to have servants as good as themselves.   Cervantes

INFIDELITY

The nurse of infidelity is sensuality.

INFLUENCE

I don't know who my grandfather was; I am much more concerned to know what his grandson will be.   Lincoln

•   •   •

If you want to influence the world pick up your pen.

INGRATITUDE

How sharper than a serpent's tooth it is
To have a thankless child!

William Shakespeare

•   •   •

A proud man is seldom a grateful man, for he never thinks he gets as much as he deserves.

Henry Ward Beecher

•   •   •

My brother was sort of odd. I remember once on his birthday he fell down a dry well. So we lowered his birthday cake to him. He didn't even tug on the rope to say thanks.

INK

One drop of ink will make millions think.

IN-LAWS

Advice squad.

•   •   •

Men speak of their in-laws as if their wives didn't have any.

INSANE

"How do you know that man who shot himself was insane?"

"He had two teeth filled an hour before he did it."

INSANE ASYLUM

A home for old joke book writers.

INSANITY

Insanity is hereditary: you can get it from your children.

Sam Levenson

•   •   •

Insanity destroys reason, but not wit.

•   •   •

In a traffic court, a college student was summoned to the bench. The clerk read the charge, "Parking in a no-parking zone," and the judge asked the young man how he pleaded, guilty or not guilty.

"Insanity, your honor," the student responded.

Startled, the judge looked up. "Insanity?" he echoed.

"Yes, sir," the young man said

earnestly. "I must have been insane to park there because I don't have the money to pay the fine."

Choking back his laughter, the judge gave the student a lecture on parking in no-parking zones — and assessed him court costs.

INSECURE

Mother of small boy to child psychiatrist: "Well, I don't know whether or not he feels insecure, but everybody else in the neighborhood certainly does!"

INSOMNIA

Student One: I think I'm getting insomnia.
Student Two: Why?
Student One: I woke up twice in chemistry class today.

INSTALLMENT BUYING

A system that makes the months shorter and the years longer.

INSTANT REPLAY

Walter: As soon as my wife and I start to quarrel, my wife becomes historical.
Charlie: You mean, hysterical?
Walter: No, she rakes up the past.

INSTRUMENT

One of the most difficult instruments to play well is second fiddle.

INSULT

There are two insults no human being will endure: that he has no sense of humor, and that he has never known trouble. Sinclair Lewis

• • •

"One of your guests insulted me!"

"Only one?"

• • •

"I hear you were out dining in a swell home last night?"

"Yes, just as we sat down at the table, the host insulted me. I got so mad that I left right after the supper."

INSURANCE

Jack: Don't you know you can't sell insurance without a license?
Buck: I knew I wasn't selling any but I didn't know the reason.

INTERFERING

Yanking a dog's ears is no more foolish than interfering in an argument that isn't any of your business.   Proverbs 26:17

INTEREST

I don't believe in principle, but I do in interest.

INTELLIGENT

The intelligent man is always open to new ideas. In fact, he looks for them.   Proverbs 18:15

INTRODUCTION

I am not going to stand here and tell you a lot of old jokes...but I will introduce the speaker tonight who will.

I.Q.

He had an extremely high I.Q. when he was five...too bad he grew out of it.

IRONY

A taste for irony has kept more hearts from breaking than a sense of humor for it takes irony to appreciate the joke which is on oneself.

IRRITATION

Women are more irritable than men, the reason being that men are more irritating.

I.R.S.

Behind every successful man is a representative of the Internal Revenue Service.

●　　　●　　　●

Some people are always taking the joy out of life and a good many of them are in the Internal Revenue Department.

INVALID

Christy: I was an invalid once.
Lisa: You were? When was that?
Christy: When I was a baby. I couldn't walk until I was a year old.

INVENTION

Great discoveries and improvements invariably involve the co-operation of many minds. I may be given credit for having blazed the trail but when I look at the subsequent developments I feel the credit is due to others rather than to myself.

Alexander Graham Bell

INVEST

Wondering where to invest? Invest some time in your family... the dividends are great.

INVITATION

Don't demand an audience with the king as though you were some powerful prince. It is better to wait for an invitation rather than to be sent back to the end of the line,

publicly disgraced! Proverbs 25:6-7

INVOLVED

Only the person involved can know his own bitterness or joy — no one else can really share it.

Proverbs 14:10

INVOLVEMENT

Why is it that we rejoice at a birth and grieve at a funeral? It is because we are not the person involved.　　　Mark Twain

JAYWALKING

For that run-down feeling — try jaywalking.

JEALOUS

A jealous man always finds more than he looks for.

●　　　●　　　●

Crooks are jealous of each other's loot, while good men long to help each other. Proverbs 12:12

JEALOUSY

Jealousy is more dangerous and cruel than anger.　　Proverbs 27:4

●　　　●　　　●

There is more self-love than love in jealousy.　　La Rochefoucauld

●　　　●　　　●

The jealous man poisons his own banquet, and then eats it.

●　　　●　　　●

And oft, my jealousy shapes faults that are not.

William Shakespeare

●　　　●　　　●

Lots of people know a good thing the minute the other fellow sees it first.

●　　　●　　　●

There is never jealousy where there is not strong regard.

Washington Irving

JEALOUS PEOPLE

Those who suffer from poison envy.

JEST

He that would jest must take a jest,
Else to let it alone were best.

• • •

When the jest is at its best,
'Twill be well to let it rest.

• • •

A jest driven too far brings home hate.

• • •

The jest loses its point when he who makes it is the first to laugh.

• • •

Judge of a jest when you have done laughing.

• • •

Many a true word is spoken in jest.

JEWELRY

In San Francisco, there is a jewelry shop named "The Karat Patch."

JOAN OF ARC

A little boy, just back from Sunday School, asked his father if Noah had a wife.

"All the time, questions, questions, questions," replied the father. "Of course he did, Joan of Arc."

JOB

Do a disagreeable job today instead of tomorrow. You will save 24 hours of dreading to do it while having 24 hours to savor the feeling that the job is behind you.

J. O. B.

Many people nowadays have a B.A., M.A., or Ph.D. — but not always a J.O.B.

JOCKEY

Admiring
Horsewoman: "How did your horse happen to win the race?"

Jockey: "Well, I just kept whispering in his ear: 'Roses are red, violets are blue — horses that lose are made into glue!'"

JOINT

No glue will hold when the joint is bad.

JOKE

A form of humor enjoyed by some and misunderstood by most.

• • •

Thou canst not joke an enemy into a friend, but thou may'st a friend into an enemy.

• • •

Didja hear about the comic who told the same jokes three nights running — he wouldn't dare tell them standing still.

• • •

Lyricist Sammy Cahn advised a young comic: "When you're telling jokes, try your best. If that doesn't work — try somebody else's best."

• • •

When jokes give pain,
The wise abstain.

When the joke is at its best,
Then's the time to let it rest.

• • •

A mob in Montana once hanged a man because he was supposed to have stolen a horse. After quite a few hours, one of the men broke the news to the dead man's widow in this manner: "We hanged Sam for stealing a horse, but it turns out he didn't do it after all, so I guess the joke's on us."

JOURNALISM

Journalists do not live by words alone, although sometimes they have to eat them.

Adlai E. Stevenson

• • •

A journalist is a grumbler, a censurer, a giver of advice, a regent of sovereigns, a tutor of nations. Four hostile newspapers are more to be feared than a thousand bayonets.   Napoleon Bonaparte

JOY

Great joys, like griefs, are silent.

• • •

Joy is the echo of God's life within us.

• • •

If you have no joy in your religion, there's a leak in your Christianity somewhere.

Billy Sunday

JUDGE

The judge is condemned when the guilty is acquitted.

• • •

God himself, sir, does not propose to judge man until the end of his days.   Samuel Johnson

• • •

Judge not, that ye be not judged.   Matthew 7:1, KJV

JUDGMENT

Everyone complains of the bad-ness of his memory, but nobody of his judgment.

Francois de La Rochefoucauld

• • •

You shall judge of a man by his foes as well as by his friends.

• • •

Snap judgment has a way of coming unfastened.

JUDGMENT DAY

"There will be thunder, lightning, floods, fires and earthquakes!" roared the preacher, describing Judgment Day.

Wide-eyed, a little boy in the congregation tugged at his mother's sleeve: "Will I get out of school?"

JUNK

The proliferation of garage sales leads us to suspect that the whole economy is sustained by everybody else's junk.

JUSTICE

Justice is the first virtue of those who command, and stops the complaints of those who obey.

• • •

Children are innocent and love justice, while most adults are wicked and prefer mercy.

Gilbert K. Chesterton

• • •

Justice tempered with too much mercy becomes injustice.

• • •

You should defend those who cannot help themselves. Yes, speak up for the poor and needy and see that they get justice.

Proverbs 31:8, 9

KAYAK

Two Eskimos sitting in a kayak were chilly, but when they lit a fire in the craft it sank — proving once and for all that you can't have your kayak and heat it, too.

KIDS

Children would all be brought up perfectly if families would just swap kids. Everyone knows what ought to be done with the neighbor's kids.

•   •   •

One nice thing about kids is that they don't keep telling you boring stories about the clever things their parents said.

KIDNAPED

Being kidnaped and held for ransom never worries the poor man!   Proverbs 13:8

KIND

Speak kind words and you will hear kind echoes.

•   •   •

He is kind to himself who is kind to his wife.

•   •   •

A gift with a kind word is a double gift.

KINDNESS

Kindness is loving people more than they deserve.

•   •   •

Kindness goes a long ways lots of times when it ought to stay at home.

•   •   •

He that has done you a kindness will be more ready to do you another than he whom you yourself have obliged.   Benjamin Franklin

KING

Wise kings generally have wise counselors; and he must be a wise

man himself who is capable of distinguishing one.   Diogenes

•   •   •

The lion went up to the rhinoceros and asked, "Who is the king of the jungle?"

"You are, O lion," came the answer.

The lion went up to the hippopotamus and asked, "Who is the king of the jungle?"

The hippo said, "You are, O lion."

The lion went up to the elephant and asked, "Who is the king of the jungle?"

For an answer the elephant seized the lion with his trunk, threw him high in the air, caught him on the way down, and slammed him hard against a tree.

The lion arose, half dazed, shook himself, and said weakly, "Just because you don't know the right answer, you don't have to get sore."

KISS

A kiss can be a comma, a question mark, or an exclamation point.

•   •   •

What a child gets free, the young man steals, and the old man has to buy.

•   •   •

It is the passion that is in a kiss that gives to it its sweetness; it is the affection in a kiss that sanctifies it.

•   •   •

God pardons like a mother who kisses the offense into everlasting forgetfulness. Henry Ward Beecher

• • •

A peculiar proposition. Of no use to one, yet absolute bliss to two. The small boy gets it for nothing, the young man has to lie for it, and the old man has to buy it. The baby's right, the lover's privilege, and the hypocrite's mask. To a young girl, faith; to a married woman, hope; and to an old maid, charity.

• • •

Bill: Can I kiss you?
Sharon: What am I...a mind
          reader?

• • •

Girl on doorstep at the end of date: "Since we've been going dutch all evening, you kiss yourself and I'll kiss myself."

• • •

Then there was the boy who kissed his girl friend in the fog and mist.

KLEPTOMANIA

The thing about kleptomania is, if you've got it, you can always take something for it.

KNOW-IT-ALL

The only kind of person more disgusting than a know-it-all is a know-it-all who does.

KNOWLEDGE

I am not young enough to know everything.

• • •

If a little knowledge is dangerous, where is the man who has so much as to be out of danger?

• • •

He who knows but little shares it often.

• • •

He who knows but little tells it quickly.

• • •

Knowledge is a treasure, but practice is the key to it.

• • •

He who carves the Buddha never worships him.

• • •

He who knows more speaks least.

• • •

I keep six honest serving-men
(They taught me all I knew);
Their names are What and Why and When
And How and Where and Who.
                    Rudyard Kipling

• • •

All wish to possess knowledge, but few, comparatively speaking, are willing to pay the price.

• • •

He who knows not, and knows not that he knows not, is a fool. Shun him.

He who knows not, and knows that he knows not is simple. Teach him.

• • •

She knows so little and knows it fluently.

LABOR

The fruit derived from labor is the sweetest of all pleasures.

• • •

Labor is man's greatest function. He is nothing, he can do nothing, he can achieve nothing, he can fulfill nothing, without working.

LADY KILLER

Guy: I'm a lady killer.

Gal: Yeah, they take one look at you and drop dead.

LAMP

Friend: "You look all broken up. What's the matter?"

College student: "I wrote home for money for a study lamp."

Friend: "So what?"

College student: "They sent the lamp."

LANGUAGE

Language is the dress of thought.

Samuel Johnson

•   •   •

Because everyone uses language to talk, everyone thinks he can talk about language.

Johann Wolfgang von Goethe

LAST MINUTE

If it weren't for the last minute, a lot of things wouldn't get done.

LAS VEGAS

A friend of ours says he never wants to see Las Vegas again. His luck was so bad he lost his shirt in a coin laundry.

LATE

A local factory was faced with many employees coming to work late in the morning. So the President posted a bulletin on the board offering $1,000 to anyone who could come up with a solution to the problem.

The next morning one of the workers was in the President's office bright and early. "I have the perfect solution to your problem," he said. "Nobody would be late in the future."

"Sounds good," replied the President. "How do you propose to do it?"

"Let the last man to work blow the whistle."

•   •   •

Mother: "Why so late coming home from school?"

Boy: "The bus driver broke down."

•   •   •

Wife: How many times have I told you not to be late for dinner?

Husband: I don't know. I thought you were keeping score.

LAUGHTER

Those who bring sunshine to the lives of others cannot keep it from themselves.

•   •   •

Laughter is the tonic, the relief, the surcease for pain.

Charlie Chaplin

•   •   •

The young man who has not wept is a savage, and the old man who will not laugh is a fool.

George Santayana

•   •   •

A hearty laugh gives one a dry cleaning, while a good cry is a wet wash.

•   •   •

A man isn't poor if he can still laugh.

•   •   •

Laughter is the sun that drives winter from the human face.

Victor Hugo

•   •   •

I can usually judge a fellow by what he laughs at.

•   •   •

He who has the courage to laugh is almost as much master of the world as he who is ready to die.

•   •   •

Laughter cannot mask a heavy heart. When the laughter ends, the grief remains.   Proverbs 14:13

•   •   •

A laugh is worth a hundred groans in any market.

•   •   •

He who laughs — lasts.

•   •   •

Laughter — The annoying sound the other person makes when you get what you didn't have coming.

•   •   •

Belly laugh: Mirthquake.

LAW

The best way to get a bad law repealed is to enforce it strictly.

Abraham Lincoln

LAWN

Any child who is anxious to mow the lawn is too young to do it.

LAWSUIT

A bad agreement is better than a good lawsuit.

LAWYERS

Two lawyers were opposing each other for political office. "Did you tell Jake down at the barbershop that I'm a thieving, lying shyster?" asked one. "No," replied the other, "I don't know how he found out."

•   •   •

My son, a lawyer, was approached by his friend, a priest, who wanted a will drawn up. When the work was completed and ready to be mailed, my son couldn't resist inserting this note: "Thy Will Be Done."

LAZY

A lazy man sleeps soundly — and goes hungry!   Proverbs 19:15

•   •   •

"A little extra sleep, a little more slumber, a little folding of the hands to rest" — Means that poverty will break in upon you suddenly like a robber, and violently like a bandit.

Proverbs 24:33, 34

•   •   •

The lazy man is full of excuses. "I can't go to work!" he says. "If I go outside I might meet a lion in the street and be killed!"

Proverbs 22:13

•   •   •

Lazy people want much but get little, while the diligent are prospering.   Proverbs 13:4

•   •   •

A lazy man won't even dress the game he gets while hunting, but the diligent man makes good use of everything he finds.

Proverbs 12:27

LAZINESS

The mother of invention.

LEAD

He's rich. He's got gold in California, silver in New Mexico but the lead is still in the same place.

LEADERSHIP

The final test of a leader is that he leaves behind him in other men the conviction and the will to carry on. Walter Lippmann

• • •

If the blind lead the blind, both shall fall into the ditch.
Matthew 15:14, KJV

• • •

Leadership: The art of getting someone else to do something you want done because he wants to do it. Dwight D. Eisenhower

• • •

Without wise leadership, a nation is in trouble; but with good counselors there is safety.
Proverbs 11:14

• • •

Leadership is seeing the consequences of our actions further in the future than those around us can.

LEARNING

Men learn while they teach.
Seneca

• • •

He who adds not to his learning diminishes it.

• • •

Much does he gain who learns when he loses.

LEFTOVERS

The lady said to the waitress "May I have a bag to carry leftovers to my dog?"

Her 6-year-old said: "Oh, Mother, are we going to get a dog?"

LEISURE

Leisure is a beautiful garment, but it will not do for constant wear.

LEND

If you'd lose a troublesome visitor, lend him money.

LETTER

Ken: Did you hear that God was very angry with the sinfulness of man and was going to destroy all of the wicked? But before he does he sent a very special letter to all the good and righteous people. Do you know what the letter said?

Bob: No, what?

Ken: You mean you didn't get one?

LEVEE

One leg of a pair of levis.

LEVITY

My method is to take the utmost trouble to find the right thing to say, and then to say it with the utmost levity.
George Bernard Shaw

LIBBER

Did you hear about the little libber down the block — she insists that her Halloween pumpkin is a jill-o-lantern.

LIBERTY

Liberty is from God; liberties from the devil. German

• • •

Liberty doesn't work as well in practice as it does in speeches.
Will Rogers

• • •

Liberty consists in wholesome restraint. Daniel Webster

• • •

God grants liberty only to those who love it, and are always ready to guard it.   Daniel Webster

•   •   •

Liberty means responsibility. That is why most men dread it.
                    George Bernard Shaw

•   •   •

What a man exchanges for a wife.

•   •   •

Patrick Henry said: "Give me liberty or give me death." Nowadays we leave out the words liberty and death.

LIBRARY
A library is a place where the dead live.

•   •   •

In college library: "Quiet — don't disturb the strain of thought."

LICENSE
The typical American boy learns to walk within a year, and forgets how to do so immediately upon securing a driver's license.

•   •   •

The traffic officer ordered the motorist to pull up to the curb and show his driver's license — "I don't understand this, officer, I haven't done anything wrong."
"No you haven't, but you were driving so carefully I thought you might not have your license."

LIE DETECTOR
The first lie detector was made out of the rib of a man. No improvement has ever been made on the original machine.

LIES
A lie travels round the world while truth is putting on her boots.
                    C. H. Spurgeon

•   •   •

Liars should have good memories.

•   •   •

Oh, what a tangled web we weave
When first we practice to deceive!

•   •   •

One lie needs seven to wait upon it.

•   •   •

If you tell a big enough lie and tell it frequently enough, it will be believed.   Hitler

•   •   •

Lies need a great deal of killing.

•   •   •

Telling lies about someone is as harmful as hitting him with an axe, or wounding him with a sword, or shooting him with a sharp arrow.

•   •   •

Gal: You're very handsome.
Guy: Gee, I wish I could say something nice about you.
Gal: You could if you lied as well as I did.

•   •   •

Joe: How can you lie like that and look me in the face?
Moe: I'm getting used to your face.

LIFE
A front door to eternity.

•   •   •

He sins against this life, who slights the next.

•   •   •

Life is easier than you think — all you have to do is accept the impossible, do without the indispensible, and bear the intolerable. (And be able to smile at anything.)

• • •

Let us so live that when we come to die even the undertaker will be sorry.   Mark Twain

• • •

Do not take life too seriously; you will never get out of it alive.

• • •

Life is like a cash register, in that every account, every thought, every deed, like every sale, is registered and recorded.   Fulton J. Sheen

LIFESAVER
The fellow who invented the lifesaver really made a mint.

LIGHT
There is not enough darkness in all the world to put out the light of one small candle.

LIGHTNING
Lightning never strikes twice in the same place. . .it doesn't have to.

LIQUOR
The only time that liquor makes a man go straight is when the road curves.

LISTEN
It is a kingly act to listen to reason.

• • •

Before you decide
Hear the other side.

• • •

A good listener is a silent flatterer.

LISTENING
The way to tell ladies from men now that they both wear pants is the one listening is the man.

• • •

Glen: Why do women like a strong, silent man?
Brad: Because they think he's listening.

LITERATURE
Our high respect for a well-read man is praise enough of literature.
                    Ralph Waldo Emerson

LITTLE THINGS
Little leaks sink great ships.

LIVE
Let us endeavor so to live that when we come to die even the undertaker will be sorry.
                    Mark Twain

LOAFING
Employer, on payday: "Here, Jones, is your pay — for loafing seven hours."
Jones, coolly: "Excuse me — **eight** hours."

LOAFED
It is better to have loafed and lost than never to have loafed at all.   James Thurber

LOANS
Sign in a loan company office. "We serve the man who has everything but hasn't paid for it."

• • •

Loan Department officer bidding farewell to disappointed couple: "Sorry, but I hope you'll try us again sometime when you don't need it quite so badly."

• • •

It is risky to make loans to strangers!   Proverbs 20:16

● ● ●

John: Lend me fifty.
Jack: I have only forty.
John: Well, then let me have the forty and you can owe me the ten.

LOCKJAW
The best thing for bad breath.

LONELINESS
I was never less alone than when by myself.   Edward Gibbon

● ● ●

Language has created the word loneliness to express the pain of being alone, and the word solitude to express the glory of being alone.
Paul Tillich

● ● ●

The whole conviction of my life now rests upon the belief that loneliness, far from being a rare and curious phenomenon, peculiar to myself and to a few other solitary men, is the central and inevitable fact of human existence.
Thomas Wolfe

● ● ●

There are some people who not only keep you from being lonely, but make you wish you were.

LOGIC
Logic is the anatomy of thought.
John Locke

LOOPHOLE
On visiting a seriously ill lawyer in the hospital, his friend found him sitting up in bed, frantically leafing through the Bible.
"What are you doing?" asked the friend.

"Looking for loopholes," replied the lawyer.

LOSS
When wealth is lost, nothing is lost;
When health is lost, something is lost;
When character is lost, all is lost.

● ● ●

He who loses Christ is lost himself.

● ● ●

He who loses money loses much.
He who loses a friend loses more.
But he who loses faith loses all.

LOST
Hungry and exhausted, a hunter stumbled forward, throwing his arms around the man who emerged from a thicket. He cried, "Am I glad to see you! I've been lost for two days."
"What are you so glad about?" mumbled the other. "I've been lost a week!"

LOST AND FOUND
Bill: I just found this nice new penknife on the sidewalk. Someone lost it.
Dad: Are you sure it was lost?
Bill: I'm very sure. I saw the man looking for it.

LOTTERY
With snow on the way, residents of Florida may expect flurries of relatives and friends drifting up to five at a time (Bill Vaughan)...Did you hear about the fellow who won a million dollars in the lottery? The first thing he did was go home and turn up the thermostat.

LOVE

Human things must be known to be loved; but Divine things must be loved to be known.

• • •

Let him who would not be idle fall in love. Ovid

• • •

Perfect love casteth out fear.
I John 4:18, KJV

• • •

Love keeps the cold out better than a cloak. Longfellow

• • •

Love rules without a sword
And binds without a cord.

• • •

One loves more the first time, better the second.

• • •

To understand your parents' love bear your own children.

• • •

Love and a cough cannot be hid.

• • •

Absence sharpens love, presence strengthens it.

• • •

Love is love's reward.
John Dryden

• • •

And now abideth faith, hope, love, these three; but the greatest of these is love.
I Corinthians 13:13, KJV

• • •

Greater love hath no man than this, that a man lay down his life for his friends. John 15:13, KJV

• • •

Love forgets mistakes; nagging about them parts the best of friends. Proverbs 17:9

• • •

If you love somebody...tell them.

• • •

I never knew how to worship until I knew how to love.
Henry Ward Beecher

• • •

It is better to have loved and lost, than not to have loved at all.
Alfred Tennyson

• • •

If there is anything better than to be loved it is loving. Anonymous

• • •

Love at first sight keeps the divorce court busy.

• • •

Love makes fools wits, and wits fools.

• • •

Love is like an onion, you taste with delight, and when it's gone you wonder whatever made you bite!

• • •

Love your enemy and it will completely confuse him.

• • •

A man usually falls in love with the girl who asks the kind of questions he is able to answer.

• • •

Love: the delusion that one woman differs from another.
H. L. Mencken

• • •

He that falls in love with himself will have no rivals.
Benjamin Franklin

• • •

A little foolishness and a lot of curiosity.

• • •

Love is blind — and marriage is

an eye-opener.

•   •   •

Love is a three-ring circus. Engagement ring, wedding ring and suffer-ring.

•   •   •

Guy: Margie, I love you! I love you Margie!

Gal: In the first place, you don't love me; and in the second place my name isn't Margie.

•   •   •

Becky: Do you love me with all your heart and soul?

Dave: Uh-huh.

Becky: Do you think I'm the most beautiful girl in the world?

Dave: Uh-huh.

Becky: Do you think my lips are like rose petals?

Dave: Uh-huh.

Becky: Oh, you say the most beautiful things.

•   •   •

John: I can't seem to get anywhere with Jan.

Jack: What happened?

John: I told her I was knee-deep in love with her.

Jack: What was her reaction?

John: She promised to put me on her wading list.

•   •   •

Linda: Do you really love me, or do you just think you do?

Jack: Honey, I really love you...I haven't done any thinking yet.

•   •   •

Better to have loved a short man than never to have loved a tall.

LOQUACITY

He who talks much cannot talk well.   Carlo Goldoni

LUCK

I believe in luck: how else can you explain the success of those you dislike?   Jean Cocteau

•   •   •

Depend on the rabbit's foot if you will, but remember it didn't work for the rabbit.   R. E. Shay

•   •   •

I am a great believer in luck and I find the harder I work, the more I have of it.

•   •   •

Good luck is often bad luck in disguise.

LUXURY

Living in the lap of luxury isn't bad, except that you never know when luxury is going to stand up.

LYING

The liar's punishment is not in the least that he is not believed, but that he cannot believe anyone else.   George Bernard Shaw

•   •   •

A man who is caught lying to his neighbor and says, "I was just fooling," is like a madman throwing around firebrands, arrows and death!   Proverbs 26:18-19

MAGICIAN

Teacher: "I understand you're a magician. What is your favorite trick?"

Billy (the class wit): "Sawing a girl in two."

Teacher: "Marvelous! Are there any other children in your family?"

Billy: "I have ten half-sisters."

MAHARAJA

The maharaja of an Indian province decreed a ban on hunting wildlife, and soon the country was overrun with man-eating animals. When the people could stand it no longer, they gave the maharaja the heave-ho. This may be the first time in history when the reign was called on account of game.

MAJORITY

It never troubles the wolf how many the sheep may be.   Vergil

MAN

All that I care to know is that a man is a human being — that is enough for me; he can't be any worse.   Mark Twain

MANNERS

It is a mistake that there is no bath that will cure people's manners, but drowning would help.

Mark Twain

•   •   •

The toughest problem some children face is that of learning good manners without seeing any.

MANSLAUGHTER

A man charged with murder bribed a friend on the jury to hold out for a verdict of manslaughter. The jury was out for a long period of time, but at last brought in a verdict of manslaughter.

Upon visiting the prisoner the following week, the friend was thanked. "You must have had a tough time getting them to vote for manslaughter."

"Tough is right," replied the friend. "The other eleven wanted to acquit you."

MANUSCRIPT

"Here's the manuscript I offered you last year."

"Say, what's the idea of bringing that thing back here when I rejected it once?"

"You've had a year's experience since then."

MARBLEHEAD

"In Massachusetts they named a town after you."

"What is it?"

"Marblehead."

MARITAL GRAVE

Usually made with a series of little digs.

MARRIAGE

Becky, suspiciously: "I think he plans to marry me for my money."

Bob: "Well, if he does, he'll have earned it."

•   •   •

When we are married or dead, it's for a long time.

•   •   •

Man to travel agent: "We'd like to go on a pleasure cruise. Book us on different ships."

•   •   •

Whether a fellow winds up with a nest egg or a goose egg depends on the kind of chick he married.

•   •   •

Marry in a hurry, and live in a worry.

•   •   •

A deaf husband and a blind wife make a happy couple.

• • •

Talk six times with the same single lady
And you may get the wedding dress ready.   Byron

• • •

An investment that pays you dividends if you pay interest.

• • •

A man who thinks he is more intelligent than his wife is married to a smart woman!

• • •

Marriages are like diets. They can be ruined by having a little dish on the side.

• • •

One way to find out what a woman really thinks of you is to marry her.

• • •

The dumb blonde on the fifth floor says: "Marriage is really a grind. You wash dishes, make the beds — and two weeks later you have it all to do over again."

• • •

Don't marry for money; you can borrow it cheaper.

• • •

A good many things are easier said than done — including the marriage ritual.

• • •

Marriage resembles a pair of shears, so joined that they cannot be separated; often moving in opposite directions, yet always punishing any one who comes between them.

• • •

A successful marriage is an edifice that must be rebuilt every day.

• • •

Marriage is our last, best chance to grow up.   Joseph Barth

• • •

The difficulty with marriage is that we fall in love with a personality, but must live with a character.   Peter DeVries

• • •

A souvenir of love.

• • •

He who makes a bad marriage never escapes from his troubles.

• • •

Young man, you'll be troubled till you marry, and from then you'll never have rest.

• • •

Keep your eyes wide open before marriage — half shut afterwards.

• • •

Marriages may be made in heaven, but man is responsible for the maintenance work.

• • •

If a child of God marries a child of the devil, said child of God is sure to have some trouble with his father-in-law.

• • •

Marriages are made in heaven, but they are lived on earth.

• • •

Marriage is like the army...everyone complains, but you'd be surprised at how many re-enlist.

• • •

Son: Dad, I want to get married.
Dad: No, my boy, you are not wise enough.
Son: When will I be wise enough?

Dad: When you get rid of the idea that you want to get married.

• • •

Son: How much does it cost to get married, Dad?

Dad: I don't know. I'm still paying on it.

• • •

Modern marriage is like a cafeteria. A man grabs what he wants and pays for it later.

• • •

"What do you think of trial marriages?"

"I must be frank...all marriages are trial marriages."

• • •

"Can you take dictation?"

"No, I've never been married."

• • •

She calls her husband "Henry." He's the eighth.

• • •

Marriage is like a prizefight...the preliminaries are generally better than the main event.

• • •

Ken: I want to congratulate you. This is one of the happiest days of your life.

Bob: But I'm not getting married until tomorrow.

Ken: That's why I say today is one of your happiest days.

• • •

Jay: I have half a mind to get married.

Bufe: That's all you need.

• • •

Women are fools to marry men. On the other hand, what else is there to marry?

• • •

I think I am losing my mind but my wife told me it's impossible because she says I never had one.

• • •

"The man who married my mother got a prize."

"What was it?"

MARRIAGE COUNSELOR

Mr. Marriage Counselor, what can I do to help my husband get over his inferiority complex?

I keep telling him he is terrific and smart and handsome but he doesn't believe me.

Do you think the fact that I have asked for a divorce has shaken his confidence?

MARTYR

It is the cause and not merely the death tht makes the martyr.

Napoleon Bonaparte

• • •

To an unjust government a martyr is more dangerous than a rebel.

MATRIMONY

A knot tied by a preacher and untied by a lawyer.

• • •

Matrimony — the high sea for which no compass has yet been invented.

MATTERHORN

From a schoolboy's exam paper: Matterhorn was a horn blown by the ancients when anything was the matter.

MATURITY

The immature man wants to die nobly for a cause, while the mature man wants to live humanely for one.

Wilheim Stekel

MAYFLOWER

"My folks came over on the Mayflower."

"Don't feel bad about it. We can't all be born here."

MAYOR

The small daughter of a newly elected town mayor was quite proud of her father's accomplishment and was always introducing herself as "Mayor Smith's daughter." Her mother, thinking this sounded rather snobbish, instructed her to refer to herself simply as Betty Smith.

That afternoon she was playing in her front yard when a lady came by and gushed, "My goodness! You're Mayor Smith's little daughter aren't you?"

"I thought I was," replied the little girl, "but Momma says no."

MAXIM

Pithy sentences are like sharp nails which force truth upon our memory.   Denis Diderot

•   •   •

All maxims have their antagonist maxims; proverbs should be sold in pairs, a single one being but a half truth.   William Matthews

•   •   •

All the good maxims have been written. It only remains to put them into practice.

•   •   •

A good maxim is never out of season.

MEALTIME

Mealtime, as one overworked mother put it, is when the kids sit down to continue eating.

MEDICAL STUDENT

A medical student was asked how much of a certain drug should be administered to a patient. The young man replied, "Five grains."

A minute later he raised his hand. "Professor," he said, "I would like to change my answer to that question."

The professor looked at his watch and replied, "Never mind. Your patient has been dead for forty seconds."

MEDICINE

He is the best physician who is the most ingenious inspirer of hope.   Samuel Taylor Coleridge

MEDITATION

A fool is always meditating how he shall begin his life; a wise man, how he shall end it.

MEEK

Blessed are the meek for they shall inherit the earth — less 40% inheritance tax.

MERCY

He reminds me of the man who murdered both his parents, and then when sentence was about to be pronounced, pleaded for mercy on the grounds that he was an orphan.   Lincoln

MERIT

If you wish your merit to be known,

Acknowledge that of other people.   Oriental Proverb

MEMOIRS

There's nothing a man can do to improve himself so much as writing his memoirs.

MEMORIES
God gave us our memories so that we might have roses in December.

• • •

Pleasant memories must be arranged for in advance.

MEMORY
If you have to keep reminding yourself of a thing, perhaps it isn't so.   Christopher Morley

• • •

Those who cannot remember the past are condemned to repeat it.

• • •

Memory is the cabinet of imagination, the treasure of reason, the registry of conscience, and the council chamber of thought.

• • •

A liar should have a good memory.

• • •

One of the stimuli that keeps a chaperone awake is memory.

MEN
Melba: Men are all alike.
Pam: Men are all I like, too.

MENTAL BLOCK
A street on which several psychiatrists live.

MENTAL ILLNESS
Is mental illness contagious? There seems to be a lot of it going around.

MENU
American Tourist in France: "Waiter, bring me some of this — see, here on the menu."
Waiter: "Madam, the orchestra is playing it now."

• • •

At our house the menu at mealtime offers two choices — take it or leave it.

MIDDLE AGE
Middle age is when your memory is shorter, experience longer, stamina lower and your forehead higher.

• • •

In middle age you are as young as ever but it takes a lot more effort.

• • •

That time of life when we convince ourselves it's only a vitamin deficiency.

MIDGET
During the days of the Salem, Massachusetts, witch hunts, a midget was imprisoned for fortune-telling. She later escaped from jail, and the headline in the local newspaper read: SMALL MEDIUM AT LARGE.

MILK
If a cow gives milk, it need not play the piano.

MILLIONAIRE
A billionaire after taxes.

MIMEOGRAPH
I think I would have more faith in Roger's love letters if they weren't mimeographed.

MIND
I have a prodigious quantity of mind; it takes me as much as a week sometimes to make it up.
                Mark Twain

• • •

The mind is like the stomach. It is not how much you put into it that counts, but how much it digests.

•   •   •

From a wise mind comes careful and persuasive speech.

Proverbs 16:23

MINISTER

After his return from church one Sunday a small boy said, "You know what, Mommie, I'm going to be a minister when I grow up."

"That's fine," said his mother. "But what made you decide you want to be a preacher?"

"Well," said the boy pensively, "I'll have to go to church on Sunday anyway, and I think it would be more fun to stand up and yell than to sit still and listen."

MINUTES

Take care of the minutes; the hours will take care of themselves.

MIRE

Don't roll in the mire to please the pigs.

MIRROR

"I practice smiling in front of a mirror."

"I bet it works...I can't keep from laughing myself."

MIRRORS

Women were made before mirrors and they've been before them ever since.

MIRTH

A man without mirth is like a wagon without springs.

MISER

The miser and the pig are of no use till death.

•   •   •

A miser is a rich pauper.

MISERY

If misery loves company, misery has company enough.

Henry David Thoreau

MISERABLE

Many people use their youth to make their old age miserable.

MISFORTUNE

Misfortune comes on horseback, and goes away on foot.

•   •   •

The misfortunes hardest to bear are those which never come.

MISS

A miss is as good as her smile.

MISSISSIPPI

Jack: Old lady river...Old lady river...

John: No! No! Jack. The song goes "Old man river..."

Jack: Not this one. I'm singing about the Mississippi.

MISTAKE

What a doctor buries.

•   •   •

A well-adjusted person is one who makes the same mistake twice without getting nervous.

•   •   •

The greatest mistake — giving up.

MISTAKES

A man who refuses to admit his mistakes can never be successful. But if he confesses and forsakes them, he gets another chance.

Proverbs 28:13

•   •   •

He is always right who suspects that he makes mistakes.

•   •   •

In order to profit from your mistakes, you have to go out and make some.

MOCKER

A mocker stays away from wise men because he hates to be scolded.   Proverbs 15:12

•   •   •

A wise man is hungry for truth, while the mocker feeds on trash.
Proverbs 15:14

•   •   •

Punish a mocker and others will learn from his example. Reprove a wise man and he will be the wiser.
Proverbs 19:25

•   •   •

Throw out the mocker, and you will be rid of tension, fighting and quarrels.   Proverbs 22:10

MODEL

People seldom improve, when they have no other model but themselves to copy.   Goldsmith

MODESTY

The art of encouraging others to find out for themselves how important you are.

MOLEHILLS

A lot of molehills become mountains when someone adds a little dirt.

MOONSHINE

The prosecution and defense had both presented their final arguments in a case involving a Kentucky moonshiner.

The judge turned to the jury and asked: "Before giving you your instructions, do any of you have any questions?"

"Yes, Your Honor," replied one of the jurors. "Did the defendant boil the malt one or two hours, does he cool it quickly, and at what point does he add the yeast?"

MONEY

Never ask of money spent
Where the spender thinks it went.
Nobody was ever meant
To remember or invent
What he did with every cent.
Robert Frost

•   •   •

The use of money is all the advantage there is in having it.
Benjamin Franklin

•   •   •

The safest way to double your money is to fold it over once and put it in your pocket.

•   •   •

Money is a good servant, but a bad master.

•   •   •

Money lent to a friend must be recovered from an enemy.

•   •   •

Would you know what money is? Go borrow some.

•   •   •

Men get their picture on U.S. currency, but women get their hands on it.

•   •   •

It used to be a compliment to tell a man he looked as sound as a dollar. Today it's an insult.

•   •   •

No wonder it is so hard to save money. The neighbors are always buying things we can't afford.

● ● ●

...that when someone says, "It's only money," it's usually your money he's talking about.

● ● ●

Money used to talk, then it whispered. Now it just sneaks off.

● ● ●

Make all you can, save all you can, give all you can. John Wesley

● ● ●

When I have any money I get rid of it as quickly as possible, lest it find a way into my heart.

John Wesley

● ● ●

Most money is tainted. Taint yours and taint mine.

● ● ●

The easiest way to teach children the value of money is to borrow some from them.

● ● ●

Money has wings and most of us see only the tail feathers.

● ● ●

To get money is difficult, to keep it more difficult, but to spend it wisely most difficult of all.

● ● ●

If you want to know what a dollar is worth, try to borrow one.

● ● ●

Dishonest money brings grief to all the family, but hating bribes brings happiness. Proverbs 15:27

● ● ●

Mom's yearning capacity is greater than Dad's earning capacity.

● ● ●

There's something bigger than money...bills.

● ● ●

Money brings only misery. But with money you can afford it.

MONKEY

Rich: Mom, can I go to the zoo to see the monkeys?

Mother: Why, Rich, what an idea! Imagine wanting to see monkeys when your Aunt Martha is here!

MONUMENT

Deeds, not stones, are the true monuments of the great.

MORE

To have more, desire less.

MORNING

I hate mornings...they're so early.

MORTAR

Did you hear about the hod-carrier that fell two stories and covered himself with mortar? He felt mortified.

MORTGAGE

A small house is better than a large mortgage.

MOSES

Teacher: "You can be sure that if Moses were alive today, he'd be considered a remarkable man."

Lenny: "He sure ought to be, he'd be more than 2,500 years old."

MOSQUITO

The mosquito has no preference, he bites folks fat or thin.

But the welt that he raises, itches like blazes.

And that's where "the rub" comes in.

MOTHER

The mother's heart is the child's schoolroom.   Henry Ward Beecher

•   •   •

God could not be everywhere, and therefore he made mothers.

Jewish Proverb

•   •   •

The hand that rocks the cradle is the hand that rules the world.

W. S. Ross

•   •   •

Instead of asking me for a present on his 20th birthday, my son Bruce pulled a switch. He presented me with an antique gold watch. On the back were engraved the words: "To Mom, for 20 years of faithful service."

•   •   •

Every boy who has a dog should also have a mother, so the dog will be fed regularly.

MOTHER'S DAY

Mother's Day brings back memories of maternal advice and admonition. Picture the scene with these famous offspring:

Alexander the Great's mother: "How many times do I have to tell you — you can't have everything you want in this world!"

Franz Schubert's mother: "Take my advice, son. Never start anything you can't finish."

Achilles' mother: "Stop imagining things. There's nothing wrong with your heel."

Madame de Pompadour's mother: "For heaven's sake, child, do something about your hair!"

Sigmund Freud's mother: "Stop pestering me! I've told you a hundred times the stork brought you!"

MOTHER-IN-LAW

The mother-in-law frequently forgets that she was a daughter-in-law.

•   •   •

A man was told by his neighbor that his domineering mother-in-law had just died. The man remained expressionless, apparently unaffected by the news.

"Your mother-in-law has just died, and you show no expression at all?"

"If you had a toothache like I do you'd have trouble smiling, too," replied the man.

•   •   •

A married couple were having their weekly fight concerning their families.

"You never say anything nice about my family," the wife complained.

"Yes I do," her husband replied. "I said I think your mother-in-law is a lot nicer than mine."

MOTIVE

We can justify our every deed but God looks at our motives.

Proverbs 21:2

MOTIVATION

While we deliberate about beginning, it is already too late to begin.   Quintilian

MOUNTAINS

You must scale the mountains if you would view the plain. Chinese

MOUTH

A closed mouth catches no flies.

• • •

Mary's mouth costs her nothing, for she never opens it but at others' expense.

MOUSE

Teacher: Robert Burns wrote "To a Field Mouse."

Student: I'll bet he didn't get an answer.

MUD

Mud thrown is ground lost.

• • •

He who is in the mud likes to pull another in.

MULE

Cutting off a mule's ear won't make him a horse.

MUSIC

Classical music is the kind that we keep hoping will turn into a tune.

MUZZLED

A bear never knows until he is muzzled how many people are not afraid of him.

NAG

A motorist was complaining about his car. "It has a buzzer that tells me my seat belt isn't fastened, another that warns when my speed is over 55 and a light that tells me when my gas is low. My wife isn't bad enough," he continued. "Now my dashboard nags me."

NAIL

He is the kind of guy that hits the nail on the hand every time.

NAME

A person with a bad name is already half-hanged.

• • •

"A good fellow" is a costly name.

• • •

He that hath an ill name is half-hanged.

NARROW

A narrow mind and a wide mouth usually go together.

NATURE

A donkey may spend his life with horses, and yet will always bray.

NEARSIGHTED

Jack: I'm so nearsighted I nearly worked myself to death.

Elmer: What's being nearsighted got to do with working yourself to death?

Jack: I couldn't tell whether the boss was watching me or not, so I had to work all the time.

NECESSITY

Necessity is the mother of invention.   Jonathan Swift

• • •

Necessity never made a good bargain.   Franklin

NEEDS

He who buys what he needs not, sells what he needs.

NEGLECT

A little neglect may breed great mischief.   Benjamin Franklin

NEIGHBOR

Don't visit your neighbor too often, or you will outwear your welcome!"   Proverbs 25:17

• • •

Don't expect your neighbor to be better than your neighbor's neighbor.

NERVOUS
All that stops most of us from having a nervous breakdown these days is that we can't afford it.

NEUROTIC
Now there's a list of the ten most neurotic people. It's called "The Best-Stressed List."

• • •

My fourth husband is more neurotic than my third husband. I should have never left my third husband.

NEWLYWED
Newlywed couples shouldn't expect the first few meals to be perfect. After all, it takes time to find the right restaurant.

NEWS
Ill news flies fast enough.

NEXT
A fellow went to a psychiatrist and said, "Doctor, I don't know what's wrong with me. Nobody wants to talk to me. My employees don't talk to me, my children don't talk to me, my wife doesn't talk to me — why is it that nobody wants to talk to me?"

The psychiatrist said, "Next!"

NICKEL
If a nickel knew what it is worth today, it would feel like two cents.

• • •

About all you can get with a nickel these days is heads or tails.

NICKNAME
A nickname is the heaviest stone the devil can throw at a man.

• • •

A good name will wear out; a bad one may be turned; a nickname lasts forever.

NIGHT
Late-staying guest: "Well, good night. I hope I have not kept you up too late."

Yawning Host: "Not at all. We would have been getting up soon, anyway."

NIGHTMARE
What the man of a girl's dreams often turns out to be.

NOAH
As Noah remarked while the animals were boarding the Ark, "Now I herd everything."

NODDING
Following a lot of dull, long-winded speakers at a sports dinner, a well-known athlete, noticing some guests who had dozed off, started his speech: "Friends and nodding acquaintances."

NONSENSE
A little nonsense now and then,
Is relish'd by the best of men.

• • •

A little nonsense now and then
Is relished by the wisest men.

NORTH POLE
Brad: We've been at the North Pole for five months.

Charlie: Might as well stay all night.

NOSE
Cleopatra's nose: had it been shorter, the whole aspect of the world would have been altered.

Pascal

• • •

"So you had an operation on your nose?"

"Yes, it was getting so I could hardly talk through it."

NOTHING

Most of us know how to say nothing; few of us when.

• • •

Between the great things that we cannot do and the small things we will not do, the danger is that we shall do nothing.

• • •

He who begins many things finishes nothing.

• • •

He who is doing nothing is seldom without helpers.

• • •

All that is necessary
For the triumph of evil
Is that good men do nothing.
                    Edmund Burke

• • •

"What are you doing, Joe?" said I.

"Nothing, sir," was his reply.

"And you there, Tom, pray let me know?"

"I'm busy, sir — I'm helping Joe."

"Is nothing, then, so hard to do,

That thus it takes the time of two?"

"No," said the other with a smile,

And grinned and chuckled all the while;

"But we're such clever folks, d'ye see,

That nothing's hard to Joe and me."

NUDITY

Phyllis Diller says there's so much nudity in films that this year's Oscar for clothing design will probably go to a dermatologist.

OAK

On the fall of an oak, every man gathers wood.

OARS

The fellow who's busy pulling on the oars hasn't got time to rock the boat.

OBEDIENCE

He that hath learned to obey will know how to command.

• • •

There are two kinds of men who never amount to much: those who cannot do what they are told, and those who can do nothing else.

• • •

One of the first things one notices in a backward country is that children are still obeying their parents.

• • •

God blesses those who obey Him; happy the man who puts his trust in the Lord.   Proverbs 16:20

OBESITY

Obesity in this country is really widespread.

OBEY

She: In most marriage ceremonies they don't use the word "obey" anymore.

He: Too bad, isn't it. It used to lend a little humor to the occasion.

• • •

He that cannot obey, cannot command.

OBLIGATION

Don't associate with (become obligated to) evil men; don't long for their favors and gifts. Their kindness is a trick; they want to use you as their pawn. The delicious food they serve will turn sour in your stomach and you will vomit it, and have to take back your words of appreciation for their "kindness." Proverbs 23:6-8

OBOE

An English tramp.

OBSCENE

What is this world coming to? I hear they just arrested a fellow who talks dirty to plants. Caught him making an obscene fern call!

OBSERVANT

Did you hear about the observant chap who claims to have discovered the color of the wind? He went out and found it blew.

OBSTACLE

An obstacle is often an unrecognized opportunity.

OCEANOGRAPHY

Oceanography is research in depth.

OFFENSE

It is harder to win back the friendship of an offended brother than to capture a fortified city. His anger shuts you out like iron bars.
Proverbs 18:19

OIL

A little oil may save a deal of friction.

OLD AGE

More people would live to a ripe old age if they weren't too busy providing for it.

● ● ●

Young man: Why did you live to be the age of 115?

Old man: Mainly because I was born in 1861.

OLD FOLKS

We old folks know more about being young than young folks know about being old.

OLD MAID

Slipping beauty.

OLD MAID'S LAUGHTER

He! He! He!

OLD-TIMER

One who remembers when people who wore blue jeans worked.

● ● ●

You're an old-timer if you remember when the only babes politicians kissed were those in their mother's arms.

● ● ●

You are an old-timer if you remember when a babysitter was called Mother.

OLYMPICS

"He should be in the Olympics, the way he jumps to conclusions."

ONE-TRACK

Most people operate on a one-track mind of two rails — "ME" and "I".

OPERATION

Operations are so common these days that you can hardly work yours into the conversation unless it is fatal.

● ●

He has had so many operations that they are going to put on a swinging door next time.

OPERETTA

Question: What is an operetta?
Answer: A girl who works for the telephone company.

OPINION

You've no idea what a poor opinion I have of myself, and how little I deserve it.

• • •

People do not seem to realize that their opinion of the world is also a confession of character.

Ralph Waldo Emerson

• • •

Poll-taker to boss: "Our latest opinion poll showed 90 percent of the people aren't interested in the opinions of other people."

• • •

We ask for information, but are interested mostly in what confirms our opinion.

OPPORTUNITY

Opportunities always look bigger going than coming.

• • •

Lots of people know a good thing the minute the other fellow sees it first.

• • •

The doors of opportunity are marked "Push" and "Pull."

• • •

Opportunity is frequently overlooked because it disguises itself as work.

• • •

The opportunity of a lifetime is seldom so labelled.

• • •

A wise man will make more opportunities than he finds. Bacon

• • •

The commonest form, one of the most often neglected, and the safest opportunity for the average man to seize, is hard work.

• • •

When your automobile engine develops a knock, chances are it's opportunity knocking for some mechanic.

• • •

The trouble with opportunity is that it comes disguised as hard work.

OPPRESSION

You can't hold a man down without staying down with him.

Booker T. Washington

• • •

He who gains by oppressing the poor or by bribing the rich shall end in poverty. Proverbs 22:16

OPTIMIST

"Twixt optimist and pessimist
The difference is droll;
The optimist sees the donut
The pessimist the hole."

• • •

Question: What do they call a man who runs the motor of his car while waiting for his wife?
Answer: An optimist.

ORATORS

What the orators want in depth, they give you in length.

ORDEAL

What some ideal marriages turn out to be.

ORDER

Two dangers constantly threaten the world: order and disorder.

• • •

Let all things be done decently and in order.

ORGANIZED

Don't confuse this confusion with disorganization...because we're not that organized yet.

ORIGINALITY

Originality is nothing but judicious imitation.

• • •

Many a man fails as an original thinker simply because his memory is too good.

• • •

Originality is undetected plagiarism.

ORTHOPEDIST

Orthopedists get all the breaks.

OTHERS

You can't spell "brothers" and not spell "others."

OVERDRAWN

Husband: I just got a notice from the bank saying I'm overdrawn.

Wife: Try some other bank ...they can't all be overdrawn.

OVEREATING

The only thing harder than giving up overeating is trying to keep from telling everyone how you did it.

OX

Some cannot manage the calf and still want to carry the ox.

PAIL

God gives the milk but not the pail.

PAINT

Over bench: "Wet paint. Watch it or wear it."

PALM

Sally: "Well, I'm falling in love and I think I should go to a palmist or a mind reader. Which would you suggest?

Hallie: "You'd better go to a palmist — you know you've got a palm."

PANHANDLER

A fellow walked up to a panhandler and politely remarked: "You're not too old and you look reasonably fit. Why don't you try to get a job?"

"I can't. I inherited this business from my father!"

PANTYHOSE

One father to another: "My daughter is in that awkward age. She tore her pantyhose while hunting Easter eggs."

PAPERWEIGHTS

A London street-market vendor posts this sign at his stall: "Lovely glass paperweights! The only way to keep housekeeping bills down!"

PARAFFIN

Paraffin is the next order of angels above the seraphim.

PARDON

"I beg your pardon for coming so late."

"My dear, no pardons are needed. You can never come too late."

PARENTS

The first half of our lives is ruined by our parents and the second half by our children.

Clarence Darrow

• • •

The most important thing a father can do for his children is to love their mother.

• • •

We never know the love of the parent till we become parents ourselves.   Henry Ward Beecher

• • •

Advice to parents: Don't be hard on the children when they fight; they may be just playing house.

• • •

Parents spend the first part of a child's life getting him to walk and talk, and the rest of his childhood getting him to sit down and shut up.

PARTING

Two partners had come to the parting of the ways over social and business differences.

"You stole my accounts," shouted one. "You crook."

"And you stole my wife," shouted the other. "You horse thief."

PARTY

I am not a member of any organized party — I am a Democrat.   Will Rogers

PASSION

Passion makes idiots of the cleverest men, and makes the biggest idiots clever.

Francois de La Rochefoucauld

PASTOR

"The pastor teaches, though he must solicit his own classes. He heals, though without pills or knife. He is sometimes a lawyer, often a social worker, something of an editor, a bit of a philosopher and entertainer, a salesman, a decorative piece for public functions, and he is supposed to be a scholar. He visits the sick, marries people, buries the dead, labors to console those who sorrow and to admonish those who sin, and tries to stay sweet when chided for not doing his duty. He plans programs, appoints committees when he can get them; spends considerable time in keeping people out of each other's hair; between times he prepares a sermon and preaches it on Sunday to those who don't happen to have any other engagement. Then on Monday he smiles when some jovial chap roars, what a job — one day a week!"

PATIENCE

Everything comes to him who hustles while he waits.

Thomas A. Edison

• • •

Patience is bitter, but its fruit is sweet.   Rousseau

• • •

Beware the fury of a patient man.   John Dryden

• • •

It is easy finding reasons why other folks should be patient.

• • •

An ounce of patience is worth a pound of brains.

• • •

It's important that mothers with small children save something for a rainy day — patience.

• • •

Patience is the ability to stand something as long as it happens to the other fellow.

• • •

He that hath no patience hath nothing at all.

• • •

With patience I the storm sustain,
For sunshine still doth follow rain.

• • •

The world is his who has patience.

• • •

The secret of patience is doing something else in the meantime.

PATHETIC

Veteran comedian George Burns told a TV audience: "I can do anything at 80 that I could do at 18 — which just goes to show you how pathetic I was at 18."

PATRIOTISM

Ask not what your country can do for you.

Ask what you can do for your country. John Fitzgerald Kennedy

PAWS

Velvet paws hide sharp claws.

PAY

If you pay your servant badly, he will pay himself.

PAYMENT

He who dances must pay the fiddler — also the waiter and the porter, the hat check girl, the doorman, and the parking lot attendant.

PAYMENTS

Rod: I've got the worst kind of car trouble anybody could have.

Ron: What kind is that?

Rod: It's when the engine won't start and the payments won't stop.

PEANUT BUTTER

The school cafeteria had a breakdown in the kitchen and served peanut butter and jelly sandwiches instead of the usual hot meal. After lunch a satisfied second grader complimented the cafeteria manager: "Finally you gave us a home-cooked meal!"

PEARLS

A pearl among pebbles is still a pearl.

• • •

In deep waters men find great pearls.

PEDIATRICIANS

Pediatricians are men of little patients.

PEEP

He who peeps through the keyhole may lose his eye.

PELTS

He that pelts every barking dog, must pick up a great many stones.

PEN

There's no wound deeper than a pen can give,

It makes men living dead, and dead men live.

PENDULUM
A pendulum travels much, but it only goes a tick at a time.

PERCEPTION
The heart has eyes which the brain knows nothing of.

PERENNIALS
The Sunday after Easter our minister got up and looked over the congregation, which was quite a bit smaller than the previous week, and said, "Well, I see the Easter lilies are gone, but the perennials are still here."

PERFECTION
If a man should happen to reach perfection in this world, he would have to die immediately to enjoy himself.   Josh Billings

●   ●   ●

Trifles make perfection, and perfection is no trifle. Michelangelo

PERFORMER
He isn't the kind of a performer that 'stops a show'...but I have often seen him 'slow it up.'

PERFUME
Anyone who thinks chemical warfare is something new doesn't know much about women's perfume.

PERPETUAL MOTION
The people in the apartment above.

PERSEVERANCE
Big shots are only little shots who keep shooting.
                Christopher Morley

●   ●   ●

Consider the postage stamp, my son. It secures success through its ability to stick to one thing till it gets there.   Josh Billings

●   ●   ●

The difference between perseverance and obstinacy is, that one often comes from a strong will, and the other from a strong won't.
                Henry Ward Beecher

PERSONAL LOAN
The reason banks refer to them as personal loans is that when you miss a payment, the banks get personal.

PESSIMIST
A pessimist is one who feels bad when he feels good for fear he'll feel worse when he feels better.

●   ●   ●

No one ought to be so pessimistic he can't see some good in the other fellow's troubles.

●   ●   ●

A person who grows their own crab grass.

●   ●   ●

A lot of pessimists got that way from financing optimists.

●   ●   ●

A pessimist on world conditions had insomnia so bad the sheep were picketing him for shorter hours.

●   ●   ●

A pessimist complains about the noise made when opportunity knocks.

PHYSICIAN
Physician on phone: "Yes, this is the doctor. My answering service is busy at the moment."

●   ●   ●

In a California physician's waiting room: "An apple a day doesn't do it."

●　　　●　　　●

The two best physicians are Doctor Diet and Doctor Merryman.

PIANO

Wife: "I simply can't understand, John, why you always sit on the piano stool whenever we have company. Everyone knows that you can't play a note."

Husband: "I know it dear. And, as long as I'm sitting there, neither can anybody else."

PICK

"Believe me, I pick my friends."
"Yes...to pieces."

PICNIC

Man to friend: "Since I got married, life is a picnic — my wife uses paper plates."

PICTURE

A picture is a poem without words.　　　　　　Horace

●　　　●　　　●

A room hung with pictures is a room hung with thoughts.

Joshua Reynolds

PIGS

Pigs grunt about everything and nothing.

●　　　●　　　●

"He said you weren't fit to sleep with the pigs."
"And I suppose you pulled the old gag and said I was?"
"No, I stuck up for the pigs."

PILOT

The loquacious old gentleman boarded a transport plane and started a conversation with the pilot.

"This plane takes all my courage, he said, "I was almost killed twice in an airplane."

"Once would have been enough," replied the bored pilot.

PIMPLES

Question: What does one get from a goose?
Answer: Pimples.

PINCH

A man and his little girl were on an overcrowded elevator. Suddenly a lady in front turned around, slapped him and left in a huff. The little girl remarked, "I didn't like her either, Daddy. She stepped on my toe so I pinched her."

PIRATE SHIP

A pirate ship is a thugboat.

PITCH

He who pitches too high won't get through his song.

PITY

Pity costs nothing, and it ain't worth nothing.　　Josh Billings

PIZZA

Italian restaurant: "We offer you pizza and quiet."

Bennett Cerf

PLACE

The modern husband believes a woman's place is in the home — and expects her to go there immediately after work.

PLAGIARISM

About the most originality that

any writer can hope to achieve honestly is to steal with good judgment.   Josh Billings

•   •   •

A certain awkwardness marks the use of borrowed thoughts; but as soon as we have learned what to do with them, they become our own.   Ralph Waldo Emerson

•   •   •

Though old the thought and oft exprest,

'Tis his at last who says it best.

James Russell Lowell

•   •   •

When you take stuff from one writer, it's plagiarism; but when you take it from many writers, it's research.   Wilson Mizner

PLANNING

It is pleasant to see plans develop. That is why fools refuse to give them up even when they are wrong.   Proverbs 13:19

•   •   •

The wise man looks ahead. The fool attempts to fool himself and won't face facts.   Proverbs 14:8

•   •   •

Any enterprise is built by wise planning, becomes strong through common sense, and profits wonderfully by keeping abreast of the facts.   Proverbs 24:3-4

PLANTS

In potted-plant section of Fresno, California, nursery: "Please don't talk to the plants unless you're going to buy."

PLAY

Play not with a man till you hurt him, nor jest till you shame him.

•   •   •

It is better to play than do nothing.

PLEASE

Who would please all and please himself too,

Undertakes something he cannot do.

PLEASED

He is good while he's pleased, and so is the devil.

PLEASURE

What we learn with pleasure we never forget.

PLENTY

The difference between a "wise guy" and a wise man is plenty.

•   •   •

In spite of all the shortages, this is still the land of plenty. Everything you want costs plenty.

PLUMBER

Walter: Who put that statue under the sink?

Frances: That's no statue... that's the plumber.

POD

"They get along like two peeves in a pod."

POISE

The ability to be ill at ease inconspicuously.

•   •   •

Question: What is the definition of poise?

Answer: The ability to keep talking while the other guy takes the check.

POISON

"I'd like to die by poison."

"I'd like to be killed by

kindness.''

"It's easier to get poison."

POLITE

A polite man is one who listens with interest to things he knows all about when they are told to him by a person who knows nothing about them.

POLITICIAN

A politician who says he will stick to the facts has no respect for tradition.

• • •

New York cafe and restaurant owners expect a boost in business when the Democratic politicians arrive for the convention. ''Let's hope,'' says one restaurateur, ''that they spend their money the way they spend ours.''

• • •

An honest politician is one who, when he is bought, will stay bought.

POLITICS

The most promising of all careers.

• • •

Politicians are the same all over. They promise to build a bridge even where there is no river.
Nikita Khrushchev

• • •

We need a law that will permit a voter to sue a candidate for breach of promise.

• • •

All political parties die at last of swallowing their own lies.

• • •

The difference between a Republican and a Democrat is: One is IN and the other is OUT.

• • •

Some go into politics not to do good, but to do well.

• • •

There's one thing the Democrats and Republicans share in common — our money.   Woody Allen

• • •

I wish the chemists who successfully removed the lead from gasoline would try the same with our congressmen.

• • •

A lobbyist browsing through an encyclopedia the other day came upon a stunning idea. In Ancient Greece, in order to prevent idiot statesmen from passing stupid laws upon the people, at one point in Greek history lawmakers were asked to introduce all new laws while standing on a platform with a rope around their neck. If the law passed, the rope was removed. If it failed, the platform was removed.

• • •

Stepped into a men's room once and found this sign posted over one of those hot air blowers for drying hands: ''Push Button and Listen for a Short Message from the Vice President.''

• • •

After giving what he considered a stirring, fact-filled campaign speech the candidate looked out at his audience and confidently asked, ''Now, are there any questions?''

"Yes," came a voice from the rear. "Who else is running?"

POLLUTION

At lunch counter: "My new apartment has windows on all

sides, so I get cross-pollution.''

•   •   •

A lady who recently moved to Columbia after living for 48 years in New York says she loves everything about the Capital City and South Carolina, with one exception. ''How,'' she asks, with tongue in cheek, ''can you people dare breathe something you can't see? I find it a little scary myself.''

POLYGON
A heathen who has many wives.

POOR
Don't rob the poor and sick! For the Lord is their defender. If you injure them He will punish you.
Proverbs 22:22-23

POOR BOX
The minister's brain is often the ''Poor-Box'' of the church.

POPULARITY
Avoid popularity if you would have peace.   Abraham Lincoln

POSSESSIONS
The wise man carries his possessions within him.

POSITIVE
''Are you positive?''
''Only fools are positive.''
''Are you sure?''
''I'm positive.''

POSTPONED
When I was a boy, I'd rather be licked twice than postponed once.

POT
I set out in life to find the pot of gold at the end of the rainbow. Now I'm sixty and all I've got is the pot.

POT-LUCK
If you believe no two women think alike, you've never been to a pot-luck dinner.

POVERTY
A state of mind sometimes induced by a neighbor's new car.

•   •   •

I wasn't born in a log cabin, but my family moved into one as soon as they could afford it.

•   •   •

He who can bear poverty without shame deserves it.

•   •   •

A little girl who lived in a wealthy suburb was asked to write a story about a poor family and she began: ''The family was very poor. The Mommy was poor, the Daddy was poor. Brothers and sisters were poor. The maid was poor, the nurse was poor, butler was poor, cook was poor and the yardman was poor....''

•   •   •

The poor are only they who feel poor.   Emerson

•   •   •

A man can stand his own poverty better than he can the other fellow's prosperity.

•   •   •

Why do people try so hard to conceal poverty at the time they are experiencing it and then brag about is so in their memoirs?

•   •   •

He who can conceal his poverty is almost rich.

•   •   •

Some rich people are poor, and some poor people have great wealth!   Proverbs 13:7

POWER

Power will intoxicate the best hearts, as wine the strongest heads. No man is wise enough, nor good enough to be trusted with unlimited power.

PRACTICAL JOKER

A man who has a large jocular vein.

PRAISE

When we disclaim praise, it is only showing our desire to be praised a second time.
                    Francois de La Rochefoucauld

• • •

He who praises everybody, praises nobody.   Samuel Johnson

• • •

I can live for two months on a good compliment.   Mark Twain

• • •

Get someone else to blow your horn and the sound will carry twice as far.   Will Rogers

• • •

Praise: Letting off esteem.

• • •

Try praising your wife, even if it does frighten her at first.
                    Billy Sunday

• • •

It is the greatest possible praise to be praised by a man who is himself deserving of praise.

• • •

The best way to get praise is to die.

• • •

If our aim is to praise, we should forget to criticize; if our aim is to criticize, we should remember to praise.

• • •

Judicious praise is to children what the sun is to flowers.

• • •

Don't praise yourself; let others do it!   Proverbs 27:2

PRAYER

The fewer words the better prayer.   Martin Luther

• • •

If prayers were puddings, many men would starve.

• • •

Sunday School Teacher: What is prayer?
Student: That is a message sent to God at night and on Sundays when the rates are lower.

• • •

A bedtime prayer that was overheard: "I'm not praying for anything for myself...just a new bike for my brother that we can both ride."

PREACHERS

Someone who talks in another person's sleep.

• • •

One young preacher made a mistake when he encouraged his listeners to be filled with fresh veal and new zigor.

• • •

Preacher: A lot of people must be sick with colds. There was sure a great deal of coughing during my sermon this morning.
Deacon: Those were time signals.

• • •

Henry Ward Beecher asked Park Benjamin, the poet and humorist, why he never came to hear him preach. Benjamin replied, ''Why, Beecher, the fact is, I have conscientious scruples against going to places of amusement on Sunday.''

• • •

A young preacher who lost his Sunday morning sermon notes said to the audience, that he would have to depend on the Lord for the message. He went on to inform the people that if they would come back in the evening he would be better prepared.

PREACHING
The world is dying for want, not of good preaching, but of good hearing.

PREDICT
Sammy: ''Do you think anyone can predict the future with cards?''

Danny: ''My mother can. She takes one look at my report cards, then tells me exactly what will happen when my dad gets home.''

PREFERRED
Giving preferred treatment to rich people is a clear case of selling one's soul for a piece of bread.
                          Proverbs 28:21

PREJUDICE
A fox should not be of the jury at a goose's trial.   Thomas Fuller

• • •

Prejudice is a great time-saver. It enables us to form opinions without bothering with facts.

• • •

You can sway a thousand men by appealing to their prejudices quicker than you can convince one man by logic.

PREPARATION
A sensible man watches for problems ahead and prepares to meet them. The simpleton never looks, and suffers the consequences.

PRESCRIPTIONS
I finally figured out what doctors scribble on those prescriptions: ''I've got my 10 bucks, now you get yours.''

PRESENT
Historians tell us about the past. Economists predict the future. It's the present that nobody understands.

PRESIDENT
When I was a boy I was told that anybody could become President; I'm beginning to believe.
                          Clarence Darrow

• • •

Presidential error: Fordian slip.

PRETENSION
The hardest tumble a man can make is to fall over his own bluff.

PRETTY
He: The more I look at you, the prettier you get.

She: Oh?

He: I ought to look at you more often.

PRICE
If there's ever a price on your head, take it.

PRICED

Still as of old men by themselves are priced.

For thirty pieces Judas sold himself, not Christ.

PRIDE

One of the best temporary cures for pride and affection is seasickness; a man who wants to vomit never puts on airs.   Josh Billings

• • •

Pride leads to arguments; be humble, take advice and become wise.   Proverbs 13:10

• • •

Pride goes before destruction and haughtiness before a fall.
                    Proverbs 16:18

• • •

Did you hear about the man who had a gold tooth that was the pride of his life? He got in a fight the other day and someone hit him in the mouth. He had to swallow his pride.

PRIVILEGED

Under privileged: Not to have remote control for your color television set.

PROBLEMS

Opportunity in work clothes.

• • •

Why don't life's problems hit us when we are eighteen and know everything?

• • •

The best way to deal with any problem is to talk it over with three people you can trust absolutely: God, yourself and a friend.

• • •

Sufficient unto the day is the evil thereof.   Matthew 6:34, KJV

PROCRASTINATION

"Not now" becomes "never!"
                    Luther

• • •

By the street of By-and-By, one arrives at the house of Never.
                    Cervantes

• • •

A fault that most people put off trying to correct.

• • •

Procrastination is the art of keeping up with yesterday.

• • •

Sometimes we take credit for being patient when we are simply putting off doing something unpleasant.

PRODIGAL

A Sunday School class was being quizzed on the prodigal son. The teacher asked one youngster, "Who was sorry when the prodigal son returned home?"

The boy gave it a lot of deep thought, then said: "The fatted calf."

PRODUCTION

A man of words and not of deeds
Is like a garden full of weeds.

PROFESSOR

A textbook wired for sound.

PROMISES

He who promises runs in debt.

• • •

Who makes no promises has none to perform.

• • •

Bob: I would go to the end of the world for you!

Pam: Yes, but would you stay there?

PROMOTE

One-third of the people in the United States promote, while the other two-thirds provide.

Will Rogers

PROSECUTE

Notice in department store: "God may help those who help themselves — we prosecute."

PROSPERITY

Something you feel, fold and forward to Washington.

PROVERB

The ingredients of a good proverb are sense, shortness, and salt.

•   •   •

A proverb is the wit of one and the wisdom of many.

•   •   •

A proverb is good sense brought to a point.

•   •   •

A proverb is a short sentence based on long experience.

PROVOCATION

To be able to bear provocation is an argument of great reason, and to forgive it of a great mind.

John Tillotson

PRUDENCE

Good nature without prudence, is foolishness.

•   •   •

A prudent man foresees the difficulties ahead and prepares for them; the simpleton goes blindly on and suffers the consequences.

Proverbs 22:3

•   •   •

Only a simpleton believes what he is told! A prudent man checks to see where he is going.

Proverbs 14:15

PSYCHIATRIST

Rodney Dangerfield says his cousin went to a psychiatrist because he felt he was ugly. "The psychiatrist almost had my cousin convinced he wasn't ugly," the comedian said, "but he spoiled it all by making him lie on the couch face down."

•   •   •

Conversation between psychiatrist and patient:

"Now, then, what brings you to see me?"

"Doctor, you've got to help me. I am a computer programmer, and I've fallen in love with my computer. I realize, though, that I can't marry her."

"Well, I'm glad that you haven't lost your sense of reality."

"Oh, it could never work — she wants a career."

•   •   •

A man walked into a psychiatrist's office with pieces of banana around his ankles, a giant piece of gum on his head and a necklace of olives around his neck.

"Doctor," he said, "I'd like to talk to you about my brother."

•   •   •

Doctor I think perhaps you are seeing too many patients. Yesterday during our session you kept referring to me as Wilma.

Besides the fact that my name isn't Wilma, I'm not the one who is suffering from paranoid schizophrenia.

• • •

Psychiatrist: You need to get to know yourself better.

Patient: Suppose I get to know myself better and I begin to hate myself?

Psychiatrist: Impossible.

Patient: I don't know...my new wife hates me already and she's only known me for six months.

• • •

I have been coming to your counseling sessions for two years and all you do is listen to what I have to say. You never say anything back.

I didn't have to go to a psychiatrist for that. I could have stayed home with my husband. That's all he does, too.

• • •

A man walked into a doctor's office with a pelican on his head.

"You need help immediately," said the doctor.

"I certainly do," said the pelican. "Get this man out from under me."

• • •

A big-game hunter recently returned from Africa and went to a psychiatrist. He told the psychiatrist he didn't want to go through analysis, but would pay him $200 for answering two questions.

The psychiatrist said this was highly irregular, but he agreed to do it.

"Is it possible," the hunter asked, "for a man to be in love with an elephant?"

The psychiatrist said, "Absolutely impossible. In all the annals of medicine, I've never heard of it. The whole idea is ridiculous. What's your second question?"

The man then asked meekly, "Do you know anyone who wants to buy a very large engagement ring?"

• • •

Two psychiatrists met in the street. One of them kept brushing his jacket.

"What's new?" asked one.

"Nothing, really, only I have these invisible insects crawling on me?"

"Well," said the other, jumping back, "don't brush them off on me!"

PSYCHOPATH

Bob: Do you know what a psychopath is?

Bill: Sure, that's a path where psychos walk up and down.

PUN

A form of humor that causes everyone to groan and is meant to punish the hearers.

PUNCTUAL

The trouble with being punctual is that there's nobody there to appreciate it.

• • •

Nothing makes an office worker more punctual than 5 p.m.

PUNCTURE

A picture of a pun.

PUNISHMENT

If punishment reaches not the mind it hardens the offender.

•   •   •

This, it seems to me, is the most severe punishment — finding out you are wrong!   Walter Winchell

•   •   •

A wise king stamps out crime by severe punishment. Proverbs 20:26

•   •   •

Punishment that hurts chases evil from the heart. Proverbs 20:30

PUPIL

The modern pupil is one who brings the teacher a couple of aspirin tablets instead of an apple.

•   •   •

"I guess I've lost another pupil," said the professor as his glass eye rolled down the kitchen sink.

PUPPY LOVE

The beginning of a dog's life.

PURPOSE

The secret of success is constancy to purpose.   Disraeli

•   •   •

Better little talent and much purpose, than much talent and little purpose.

•   •   •

Working without method, like the pig's tail, goes all day and does nothing.

PURSE

A full purse makes the mouth run over.

PUSH

Mother: "Did you push your little sister down the stairs?"

Bobby: "I only pushed her down one step. She fell the rest of the way."

PUSHING

The reason the road to success is crowded is that it is filled with women pushing their husbands.

QUALITY

The bitterness of poor quality lingers long after the sweetness of cheap price is forgotten.

•   •   •

There is hardly anything in the world that some man cannot make a little worse and sell a little cheaper.   John Ruskin

QUARREL

He that blows the coals in quarrels he has nothing to do with has no right to complain if the sparks fly in his face.

Benjamin Franklin

•   •   •

I never take my own side in a quarrel.   Robert Frost

•   •   •

Who seeks a quarrel, finds it near at hand.

•   •   •

It takes two to have a quarrel, But only one to start it.

•   •   •

It is hard to stop a quarrel once it starts, so don't let it begin.

Proverbs 17:14

•   •   •

It is an honor for a man to stay out of a fight. Only fools insist on quarreling.   Proverbs 20:3

•   •   •

A quarrelsome man starts fights

as easily as a match sets fire to paper. Proverbs 26:21

•   •   •

As the churning of cream yields butter, and a blow to the nose causes bleeding, so anger causes quarrels. Proverbs 30:33

QUEEN
The power behind the drone.

QUESTION
He must be very ignorant for he answers every question he is asked.

•   •   •

Whoever fears to submit any question to the test of free discussion, loves his own opinion more than the truth.

•   •   •

He who asks a question is a fool for five minutes; he who does not ask a question remains a fool forever.

•   •   •

To a quick question give a slow answer.

QUIET
Very often the quiet fellow has said all he knows.

•   •   •

Quiet is what home would be without children.

•   •   •

It's only natural for older people to be quiet. They have a lot more to be quiet about.

•   •   •

Quiet people aren't the only ones who don't say much.

QUOTE
Next to the originator of a good sentence is the first quoter of it.
Ralph Waldo Emerson

•   •   •

"He who never quotes is never quoted." Frank S. Mead

RACE
A coach of a football team where they had a lot of racial problems said, "Look, there's no more black guys and no more white guys on this team. From now on everybody is one color — green." They got out on the playing field and he gave orders: "All right, all the light green guys on this side, and all the dark green ones on that side."

RADIO
Man has conquered the air but so has our neighbor's radio.

RAISE
A man asked his boss for a raise.
"But I gave you a $10 increase only last month…"
"Holy mackarel, my wife didn't tell me?"

•   •   •

Dean: "Why do you ask for a raise?"
Assistant Professor: "Well, sir, I wouldn't ask for a raise, but somehow my kids found out that other families eat three times a day."

•   •   •

"Got anything to say before I fire you?"
"Yeah…How about a raise?"

RAZOR
Jim: "I got one of those new razors that has twin blades."
Tom: "How do you like it?"
Jim: "Shaves good. But now

instead of getting nicks, I get ditto marks.''

READING

I divide all readers into two classes: those who read to remember and those who read to forget.

● ● ●

A classic is something that everybody wants to have read and nobody wants to read. Mark Twain

● ● ●

Reading is to the mind what exercise is to the body.

Joseph Addison

● ● ●

Read the best books first, or you may not have a chance to read them all.   Henry David Thoreau

● ● ●

The art of reading is to skip judiciously.

● ● ●

What you read you are. What are you reading TODAY?

● ● ●

The man who doesn't read good books has no advantage over the man who can't read them.

REAL ESTATE AGENT

The first man to make a mountain out of a molehill was probably a real estate agent.

REAL ESTATE BROKER

A real estate broker's message seen on a billboard in Oregon: ''Would you like to pay $40,000 for a $35,000 house? Wait till next year!''

REAP

Whatsoever a man soweth, that shall he also reap.

Galatians 6:7, KJV

REASON

A man always has two reasons for doing anything — a good reason and the real reason.

J. P. Morgan

● ● ●

Most of our so-called reasoning consists in finding arguments for going on believing as we already do.

REBEL

It is senseless to pay tuition to educate a rebel who has no heart for truth.   Proverbs 17:16

● ● ●

It's no fun to be a rebel's father.

Proverbs 17:21

● ● ●

A rebellious son is a grief to his father and a bitter blow to his mother.   Proverbs 17:25

● ● ●

A son who mistreats his father or mother is a public disgrace.

Proverbs 19:26

● ● ●

Don't waste your breath on a rebel. He will despise the wisest advice.   Proverbs 23:9

● ● ●

Wisdom is too much for a rebel. He'll not be chosen as a counselor!

Proverbs 24:7

● ● ●

Guide a horse with a whip, a donkey with a bridle, and a rebel with a rod to his back!

Proverbs 26:3

● ● ●

When arguing with a rebel, don't use foolish arguments as he does, or you will become as foolish as he is! Prick his conceit with silly replies! Proverbs 26:4-5

● ● ●

To trust a rebel to convey a message is as foolish as cutting off your feet and drinking poison!
Proverbs 26:6

● ● ●

Honoring a rebel will backfire like a stone tied to a slingshot!
Proverbs 26:8

● ● ●

A rebel will misapply an illustration so that its point will no more be felt than a thorn in the hand of a drunkard. Proverbs 26:9

● ● ●

The master may get better work from an untrained apprentice than from a skilled rebel!
Proverbs 26:10

● ● ●

You can't separate a rebel from his foolishness though you crush him to powder. Proverbs 27:22

● ● ●

A rebel shouts in anger; a wise man holds his temper in and cools it. Proverbs 29:11

REBUKE

A rebuke to a man of common sense is more effective than a hundred lashes on the back of a rebel. Proverbs 17:10

● ● ●

Open rebuke is better than hidden love! Proverbs 27:5

RECOUNT

A recount is when the chairman can't believe his ayes.

RED LIGHT

We went for a ride, and she went through a red light.
I said, "Didn't you see that red light?"

She said, "So what? You see one red light, you've seen them all!"

RED CROSS

Despite warnings from his guide, an American skiing in Switzerland got separated from his group and fell — uninjured — into a deep crevasse. Several hours later, a rescue party found the yawning pit, and to reassure the stranded skier, shouted down to him, "We're from the Red Cross."

"Sorry," the imperturbable American echoed back, "I already gave at the office!"

REFINISHING

An East Avon, N.Y., furniture-refinishing place is called "The Strip Joint."

REFORM

The best reformers...are those who commence on themselves.

● ● ●

The race could save on half its wasted labor
Would each reform himself and spare his neighbor.

● ● ●

Nothing so needs reforming as other people's habits. Mark Twain

REGENERATION

Every generation needs regeneration.

REINCARNATION

"Do you believe in reincarnation?"

"Yes...because nobody could be as dumb as you are in one lifetime."

● ● ●

Jack: I believe in reincarnation.

Elmer: You do?

Jack: I'll say, and when I come back to earth, I want to be a mattress.

Elmer: A mattress? Why?

Jack: So I can lie in bed all day.

REGRET

For of all sad words of tongue or pen,

The saddest are these: "It might have been!"

John Greenleaf Whittier

RELAX

The time to relax is when you don't have time for it.

RELATIVES

Inherited critics.

● ● ●

Most relatives live beyond your means.

RELIEF

My small son approached me the other day and asked if there was anything he could do around the house to earn a little pocket money.

"I can't think of anything."

"Well, then, will you put me on relief?"

RELIGION

Religion is meant to be bread for daily use, not cake for occasions.

● ● ●

Men will wrangle for religion;
Write for it;
Fight for it;
Die for it;
Anything but — live for it.

RELIGIOUS FREEDOM

To some people religious freedom means the choice of churches which they may stay away from.

REMBRANDT

"You were swindled over this Rembrandt," stated the art expert. "This picture is about 50 years old."

"Who cares how old it is," replied the proud owner, "as long as it's a genuine Rembrandt."

● ● ●

During the recent stock market dip, a broker lost everything. "I have no money to pay you," he said to his plumber, who had just given him a large bill. "Would you take a Rembrandt instead?"

"If it's got four good tires, you've got yourself a deal," replied the plumber.

REMEMBER

A worker was called on the carpet by his supervisor for talking back to his foreman. "Is it true that you called him a liar?"

"Yes, I did."

"Did you call him stupid?"

"Yes."

"Slave driver?"

"Yes."

"And did you call him an opinionated, bullheaded egomaniac?"

"No, but would you write that down so I can remember it?"

REMEMBERING

Half the fun of remembering is the rearranging.

RENT

Bill: How much are they asking for your apartment rent now?

Bob: About twice a day.

REPAIRED

Our neighbors, a young married couple, recently purchased a new car, which they treated with tender, loving care. One day, the husband backed the car into their garage and knocked the trim off the right taillight. Damage was slight, and he immediately had it repaired. A week later, the same thing happened, and he was embarrassed at the thought of bringing the car back to the shop again. His wife said lovingly, "Just say that I did it this time, dear."

"But," the husband replied sheepishly, "that's what I told them last time."

REPENTANCE

Most people repent their sins by thanking God they ain't so wicked as their neighbors.   Josh Billings

•   •   •

True repentance is to cease from sinning.

•   •   •

It is much easier to repent of sins that we have committed than to repent of those that we intend to commit.   Josh Billings

•   •   •

Late repentance is seldom true, but true repentance is never too late.

REPETITION

Like warmed-up cabbage served at each repast,

The repetition kills the wretch at last.   Juvenal

•   •   •

A man complained to a friend, "My wife Ida likes to talk things over — and over, and over, and over, and over, and over."

•   •   •

The professor of English was trying to drum into his class the importance of a large vocabulary.

"I assure you," he said, "if you repeat a word ten or twelve times, it will be yours forever."

In the back of the room a cute co-ed took a deep breath, closed her eyes and whispered, "Richard, Richard, Richard...."

REPOSE

Whilst Adam slept, Eve from his side arose:

Strange his first sleep should be his last repose.

REPRIMAND

Bill: Did you reprimand your little boy for mimicking me?

Sharon: Yes, I told him not to act like a fool.

REPROACH

To remind a man of the good turns you have done him is very much like a reproach. Demosthenes

•   •   •

The sting of a reproach is the truth of it.

REPUTATION

A reputation once broken may possibly be repaired, but the world will always keep their eyes on the spot where the crack was.

•   •   •

Associate with men of good quality if you esteem your own reputation; for it is better to be alone than in bad company.

George Washington

•   •   •

If you must choose, take a good name rather than great riches; for to be held in loving esteem is better than silver and gold.

Proverbs 22:1

• • •

What you would seem to be, be really.

• • •

Glass, china, and reputation are easily cracked, and never well mended.

• • •

It is a sign that your reputation is small and sinking, if your own tongue must praise you.

Matthew Hale

• • •

When men speak ill of these, live so that no one will believe them. Plato

• • •

No one can be caught in places he does not visit.

• • •

You can tell more about a person by what he says about others than you can by what others say about him.

• • •

A man is known by his actions; an evil man lives an evil life; a good man lives a godly life.

Proverbs 21:8

RESEMBLANCE

"Who is that homely boy who just walked into the room?"

"Why, that's my brother!"

"Oh, you must excuse me. I really hadn't noticed the resemblance."

RESIGNATION

Resignation is putting God between ourselves and our troubles.

• • •

For after all, the best thing one can do when it's raining is to let it rain. Henry Wadsworth Longfellow

RESOLUTION

Good resolutions are simply checks that men draw on a bank where they have no account.

Oscar Wilde

RESPONSIBILITY

The highest praise for a man is to give him responsibility.

• • •

One way to keep a man's feet on the ground is to put a heavy responsibility on his shoulders.

• • •

When some people are given responsibility, they grow; others merely swell.

RESTAURANT

Man in restaurant: "I'll have the $5.00 dinner."

Waitress: "Would you like that on white or dark bread?"

• • •

Restaurant chains: Cook-alikes.

RESULT

Results! Why, man, I have gotten a lot of results. I know several thousand things that won't work. Thomas A. Edison

RESURRECTION

Christianity is a religion of the open tomb.

RETIREMENT

I'll take any job that gets me out of the house. My husband retired yesterday.

• • •

Elderly clerk approached the personnel manager with some reluctance. "I suppose I'd better retire soon. My doctor tells me my hearing is going fast and I notice I don't hear what some of the customers say to me."

"Retire? Nonsense! I'll put you in the complaint department."

• • •

Don't think of retiring from the world until the world will be sorry that you retire. I hate a fellow whom pride or cowardice or laziness drives into a corner, and who does nothing when he is there but sit and growl. Let him come out as I do, and bark.   Samuel Johnson

• • •

The best time to start thinking about your retirement is before the boss does.

• • •

A man is known by the company that keeps him on after retirement age.

RETORT
As surely as a wind from the north brings cold, just as surely a retort causes anger! Proverbs 25:23

RETROACTIVE
Wedded Blitz. This letter-to-the-editor appeared in a local newspaper: "I have read recently that the word 'obey' is now being omitted from the wedding ceremony. May I ask if you think the new wording for the wedding service is retroactive?"

REVENGE
The best revenge is to prevent the injury.

• • •

Recompense to no man evil for evil.   Romans 12:17, KJV

• • •

You are not permitted to kill a woman who has injured you, but nothing forbids you to reflect that she is growing older every minute. You are avenged 1440 times a day.

REVENUE
Internal Revenue man, eyeing taxpayer's expense claims: "Shall we go over this item by item or would you prefer to chicken out right now?"

REVERENCE
Reverence for God gives a man deep strength; his children have a place of refuge and security.
    Proverbs 14:26

REVERSE REASON
She married him because he was such a "dominating man," she divorced him because he was such a "Dominating male."

He married her because she was so "fragile and petite," he divorced her because she was so "weak and helpless."

She married him because "he knows how to provide a good living," she divorced him because "all he thinks about is business."

He married her because "she reminds me of my mother," he divorced her because "she's getting more like her mother every day."

She married him because he was "gay and romantic," she divorced him because he was "shiftless and fun-loving."

He married her because she was

"steady and sensible," he divorced her because she was "boring and dull."

She married him because he was "the life of the party," she divorced him because "he never wants to come home from a party."

REVIEWS
"She not only reads her husband like a book, she gives the neighbors reviews."

REVOLUTION
Every revolution was first a thought in one man's mind.

RHUBARB
Question: What is another name for rhubarb?
Answer: Bloodshot celery.

RICH
Beverly: A scientist says that what we eat we become.
Melba: Oh, boy. Let's order something rich.

• • •

Trying to get rich quick is evil and leads to poverty.
Proverbs 28:22

• • •

Better to live rich than to die rich.

• • •

God help the rich, for the poor can beg.

RICHES
Don't weary yourself trying to get rich. Why waste your time? For riches can disappear as though they had the wings of a bird!
Proverbs 23:4-5

RICH RELATIVES
The kin we love to touch.

• • •

Question: What type of person lives the longest?
Answer: A rich relative.

RIDE
Two men ride a horse, one must ride behind.

RIDICULE
Ridicule is the first and last argument of fools.

RIGHT
The trouble with doing something right the first time is that nobody appreciates how difficult it was.

RIGHTS
A man is endowed with certain inalienable rights all of which he must fight for.

• • •

The good man knows the poor man's rights; the godless don't care.
Proverbs 29:7

• • •

Every right implies a responsibility; every opportunity, an obligation; every possession, a duty.

RISK
I've run less risk driving my way across country than eating my way across it.
Duncan Hines

ROBBED
The teller had just been robbed for the third time by the same man, and the police officer was asking if he had noticed anything specific about the criminal.

"Yes," said the teller, "he seems to be better dressed each time."

ROBIN HOOD

Talk like Robin Hood when you can shoot his bow.

ROD

Fuller said: "He that will not use the rod on his child, his child shall be used as a rod on him."

ROME

Buck: Haven't you heard of the fall of Rome?

Nancy: No, but I remember hearing something drop.

ROOKIE

First Rookie: "I feel like punching that top sarge in the nose again!"

Second Rookie: "What do you mean, again?"

First Rookie: "Well, I felt like it yesterday, too."

ROT

When there is moral rot within a nation, its government topples easily; but with honest, sensible leaders there is stability.

Proverbs 28:2

RUBBER BAND

In the bank one day the little moron suddenly called out at the top of his voice, "Did anyone drop a roll of bills with a rubber band around it?"

Several people at different tellers' windows answered, "I did!"

"Well, I just now found the rubber band," said the little moron.

RUDDER

He who will not answer to the rudder, must answer to the rocks.

• • •

The first hour of the morning is the rudder of the day.

H. W. Beecher

RUMMAGE SALE

Many husbands go to church rummage sales to buy back their Sunday pants.

RUMOR

A rumor goes in one ear and out many mouths.

• • •

Rumor is one thing that gets thicker as you spread it.

• • •

There is no such thing as an idle rumor.

• • •

What dainty morsels rumors are. They are eaten with great relish!

Proverbs 18:8

RUN

Better a good run than a long standing.

RUSH HOUR

When the traffic stands still.

RUST

A sword, a spade and a thought should never be allowed to rust.

SABLE

The skin girls love to touch.

SABOTEUR

A lazy man is brother to the saboteur.   Proverbs 18:9

SAIL

Don't carry too much sail.

SALESMAN

Brad: I'm an independent

salesman.

Dave: Really?

Brad: Yes...I take orders from no one.

SALT

A small boy was watching his mother change the baby. When she overlooked sprinkling the tot's backside with talcum powder and hurried him into his diaper, the five-year-old reproved her sharply, "Hey, Mom, you forgot to salt him."

SANDBAR

"I've been running boats on this river so long, I know where every sandbar is," boasted the steamboat pilot.

Just then the boat ran aground.

"There," he said, "that's one of them now."

SANTA CLAUS

The three stages of man: he believes in Santa Claus; he does not believe in Santa Claus; he is Santa Claus.

SAP

Even the best family tree has its sap.

SARCASM

Sarcasm is jealousy in bold disguise.

●　　　●　　　●

Sarcasm — getting an edge in wordwise.

●　　　●　　　●

Sarcasm: quip lash.

SATAN

Satan as a master is bad, his work worse, his wages worst of all.

SATIRE

Strange! That a man who has wit enough to write a satire should have folly enough to publish it.

SATISFACTION

Telling the truth gives a man great satisfaction, and hard work returns many blessings to him.

Proverbs 12:14

SATISFIED

Lawyer: (Handing check for $100 to client who had been awarded $5,000). There's the balance after deducting my fee. What are you thinking of? Aren't you satisfied?

Client: I was just wondering who got hit by the car, you or me?

SAVER

A saver grows rich by seeming poor, a spender grows poor by seeming rich.

SAXOPHONE

The music professor in a small town met Pop Parker on the street, carrying a long music case.

Professor: "Oh, Mr. Parker, I see you've bought a saxophone."

Pop Parker: "No, I just borrowed it from the man next door."

Professor: "But why did you want to do that? You can't play it, can you?"

Pop Parker: "No, but neither can the man next door, while I've got it.

●　　　●　　　●

"Does my practicing make you nervous?" a saxophone player asked his neighbor.

"It did when you first moved in" replied the neighbor, "but now I don't care what happens to you."

SCAFFOLDING

Ken: My uncle fell off a scaffolding and was killed.

Bob: What was he doing up on the scaffolding?

Ken: Getting hanged.

SCHOOL

Teacher: Why are you crying?

Student: I'm crying because school bores me and I have to stay here until I'm at least 17.

Teacher: Don't let that worry you. I have to stay here until I'm 65.

● ● ●

"All that criticism of the American school system in newspapers and magazines is completely justified," exclaimed a teenage girl just home from school.

"Do you really think so?" asked her mother.

"Yes, I do," replied the girl. "And if you want proof of how bad it is, just look at the terrible marks on this report card."

● ● ●

Teacher: You there in the back of the room: what was the date of the signing of the Magna Charta?

Man: I dunno.

Teacher: You don't know. Well, what were the dates of the Third Crusade?

Man: I dunno.

Teacher: Indeed. I assigned this work last Friday. What were you doing last night?

Man: I was out to a party with some friends. Didn't get home until five a.m.

Teacher: And you have the audacity to stand there and tell me that! Just how do you expect to pass this course?

Man: I dunno, mister. I just come in to fix the radiator.

SCHOOL DAYS

School days are the best days of your life...provided your children are old enough to go.

SCRATCH

Pull the cat's tail, and she'll scratch without fail.

● ● ●

A man called for jury duty asked the judge to be dismissed because he was ill. The judge inquired what was wrong with him.

"I have the seven-year-itch, your Honor," he replied.

The judge turned to the clerk of court and said, "Scratch this man."

SCRATCHING

A teacher called on the mother of a boy who came to school in a dirty condition.

"Can you explain," she asked, "how he gets his nails so dirty?"

"I expect that's because he's

always scratching himself," replied the fond mother.

SEAFOOD

The president of a chain of seafood specialty restaurants is known by his associates as The Codfather.

SEASICK

Question: What's green, has two legs, and a trunk?

Answer: A seasick traveler.

SECRET

Women keep a secret well but sometimes it takes quite a few of them to do it.

•   •   •

If you wish another to keep your secret, just keep it yourself. Seneca

•   •   •

What we give to others to keep for us.

•   •   •

A secret known to be concealed,
Like money suspected in a field,
Is half discovered.

•   •   •

Some people's idea of keeping a secret is to refuse to tell who told it to them.

•   •   •

Some people always think it takes two to keep a secret.

•   •   •

Three may keep a secret, if two of them are dead.   Franklin

•   •   •

If you **really** want to keep a secret, you don't need any help.

•   •   •

A secret is a weapon and a friend.

SECRETARY

One of them said, "All I asked the boss was, 'Do you want the carbon copy double spaced too?'"

SECRETIVE

Teacher: In your homework last night, what did you find out about the salivary glands?

Student: I couldn't find out a thing. They're so secretive.

SECURITY

If a king is kind, honest and fair, his kingdom stands secure.

SELF-CONTROL

Keep yourself from the opportunity and God will keep you from the sins it leads to.

•   •   •

Greater is he who conquers himself than he who conquers a thousand.

•   •   •

It is better to be slow-tempered than famous; it is better to have self-control than to control an army.   Proverbs 16:32

•   •   •

A man without self-control is as defenseless as a city with broken-down walls.   Proverbs 25:28

SELF-IMPROVEMENT

People seldom improve when they have no other model but themselves to copy after.

Oliver Goldsmith

SELFISH

SEL-FISH is the most dangerous fish existing.

SELFISHNESS

He who lives only to benefit

himself confers on the world a benefit when he dies.   Tertullian

•   •   •

The man who lives by himself and for himself is likely to be corrupted by the company he keeps.   Charles H. Parkhurst

SELF-KNOWLEDGE

When you decide to know yourself, you may find the acquaintance isn't worth the effort.

•   •   •

To know yourself well, is to esteem yourself little.

SELL

Judas sold Christ for $16.41. A lot of people sell him for much LESS and then fail to collect.

SENATORS

Rome had senators, that's why it declined.

SENSE

We hardly find any persons of good sense save those who agree with us.   La Rochefoucauld

•   •   •

The ability to say nay.

•   •   •

There are forty men of wit to one man of sense.

•   •   •

Good sense is a thing all need, few have, and none think they want.

SENSIBLE

A sensible son gladdens his father. A rebellious son saddens his mother.   Proverbs 15:20

•   •   •

Bill: You look like a nice, sensible, well-adjusted girl. Let's go steady.

Sharon: No. I'm just as nice, sensible, and well-adjusted as I look.

SENTENCE

Judge: Twenty days or twenty dollars.
Prisoner: I'll take the money, Your Honor.

SEPARATES

The thing that separates the men from the boys is the price of auto insurance.

SEPARATION

Bob: Time separates the best of friends.
Bill: So does money.
Ken: And don't forget marriage!

SERMON

A sermon's length is not its strength.

•   •   •

One beautiful Sunday morning, a minister announced to his congregation: "My good people, I have here in my hands three sermons — a $100 sermon that lasts five minutes, a $50 sermon that lasts 15 minutes and a $10 sermon that lasts a full hour. Now, we'll take the collection and see which one I'll deliver."

•   •   •

The average man's idea of a good sermon is one that goes over his head — and hits one of his neighbors.

SERVANT

A servant is best discovered by his master's absence.

•   •   •

He that is greatest among you

shall be your servant.

Matthew 23:11, KJV

• • •

A king rejoices in servants who know what they are doing; he is angry with those who cause trouble.

Proverbs 14:35

• • •

A servant's heart, is becoming exciting about making someone else successful.

• • •

A good servant makes a good master.

SERVICE

A man who had been married for ten years was consulting a marriage counselor, "When I was first married, I was very happy. I'd come home from a hard day down at the shop, and my little dog would race around barking, and my wife would bring me my slippers. Now everything's changed. When I come home, my dog brings me my slippers, and my wife barks at me."

"I don't know what you're complaining about," said the counselor. "You're still getting the same service."

• • •

He who serves well need not fear to ask his wages.

SETTLED

Judge: "Couldn't this have been settled out of court?"

Defendant: "Your Honor, that is exactly what we were doing but a couple of police-

men butted in and stopped the fight."

SEWAGE

The Red Sea and the Mediterranean are connected by the Sewage Canal.

SHADOW

Don: I'm afraid of my shadow.

Art: You ought to be...you look like a crowd is following you.

SHARE

Why is it a woman is willing to share her whole life with her husband — but not her closet space?

SHAZAMM

Question: What is red and goes "Shazamm?"

Answer: Captain Cherry.

SHIP

A ship in harbor is safe, but that is not what ships are built for.

• • •

"It's no use waiting for your ship to come in unless you have one out."

SHIPS

All girls are like ships. If kept in good shape and painted frequently, they stay see-worthy.

SHOCK

Cross an electric eel with a sponge and you'll have shock absorbers.

SHOE REPAIR

While rummaging through his attic, a man found a shoe repair ticket that was nine years old. Figuring that he had nothing to lose, he went to the shop and presented the ticket to the proprietor, who reluctantly began a search for the unclaimed shoes. After ten minutes, the owner reappeared and handed back the ticket.

"Well," asked the customer, "did you find the pair?"

"Yes," replied the shop owner. "They'll be ready Tuesday."

SHOES

Hotel clerk in big city: "Why don't you wipe the mud off your shoes when you come in here?"

Hillbilly: "What shoes?"

SHOPPING

Grocery shopping: Staple chase.

SHORT CUT

A short cut is often the longest way.

SHORTEN

Kissing shortens life...single life.

SHIRT-SLEEVE

People who wear short-sleeve shirts can't make off-the-cuff remarks.

SHORT-TEMPERED

A short-tempered man is a fool. He hates the man who is patient.
Proverbs 14:17

• • •

Keep away from angry, short-tempered men, lest you learn to be like them and endanger your soul.
Proverbs 22:24-25

SHOT

"I shot my dog."

"Was he mad?"

"Well, it didn't seem to exactly please him."

SICKNESS

Sickness has four stages: ill, pill, bill, will.

• • •

I hope I'm really sick. I'd hate to feel like this if I'm well.

SIDE

Sir, my concern is not whether God is on our side; my great concern is to be on God's side, for God is always right.   Lincoln

SIEVE

Said the sieve to the needle, "you have a hole in your head."

SIGN

A dollar sign has been described as a capital S which has been double-crossed.

• • •

"What sign were you born under?"

"Quiet — Hospital Zone."

• • •

Outside a house in Sussex, England: "Beware of owner. Never mind the dog."

• • •

Sign outside of house rented by gypsies:
FORTUNES TOLD: $2.00: PSYCHOANALYSIS 75 CENTS EXTRA.

• • •

Sign in store window:
FRESH EGGS PACKED IN NO-DEPOSIT, NO-RETURN, BIODEGRADABLE SHELLS.

• • •

Sign outside house in the city:
TRESPASSERS WILL BE PROSECUTED TO THE FULL EXTENT OF ONE GERMAN SHEPHERD.

• • •

Sign on garbage truck:
SATISFACTION GUARAN-
TEED, OR DOUBLE YOUR GAR-
BAGE BACK.

SIGN LANGUAGE

Myrlene: What do you think
we should give Bob
for his wedding pres-
ent?

John: A book on sign lan-
guage.

SILENCE

Sometimes silence is not golden
— just yellow.

• • •

If you keep your mouth shut you
will never put your foot in it.

• • •

Silence is foolish if we are wise,
but wise if we are foolish.

• • •

Silence is one of the hardest
arguments to refute. Josh Billings

• • •

Talking comes by nature, silence
by wisdom.

• • •

Most people are quite happy to
suffer in silence, if they are sure
everybody knows they are doing it.

• • •

You hesitate to stab me with a
word,
And know not silence is the
sharper sword.

• • •

Silence is the only substitute for
brains.

• • •

As we must account for every
idle word, so must we for every idle
silence.

• • •

No one is so hard to answer as a
fellow who keeps his mouth shut.

• • •

Silence is sometimes the severest
criticism.

• • •

The only substitute for wisdom
is silence.

SIMPLETON

The wise man learns by listening; the simpleton can learn only
by seeing scorners punished.
Proverbs 21:11

SIN

He who is without sin among
you, let him be the first to throw a
stone at her. John 8:7, NAS

• • •

Confess your sins to the Lord,
and you will be forgiven; confess
them to men, and you will be
laughed at. Josh Billings

SINGER

A folk singer is a person who
gets rich singing about how wonderful it is to be poor.

SINKING FUND

We had a sinking fund. It just
went down for the third time.

SKEPTICISM

Skeptics are never deceived.

SKILLFUL

Learn of the skillful: he that
teaches himself hath a fool for a
master.

SKIN

Most women have skin they love
to retouch.

SLACKS

Another proof that women wear pants in the family.

SLEEP

A clothing manufacturer, so worried that he couldn't sleep, was advised by his business associates to count sheep. Next day the man appeared more exhausted than ever. "Sure, I counted sheep," he told his associates. "I counted up to 20,000. Then I began figuring: Those 20,000 sheep would produce 80,000 pounds of wool — enough to make 30,000 yards of cloth. That would make 12,000 overcoats. Man! Who could sleep with an inventory like that?"

SLEEPING PILLS

The new bride stopped at the druggist's for a refill of an order of sleeping pills. "I don't know what I'd do without them. I'd never get any rest."

"Be sure not to take too many," cautioned the druggist.

"Me?" said the bride in surprise. "Oh, I never take them. I give them to my husband."

SLEET

Slip cover.

SLOW

"Look here, private, this man beside you on this fatigue detail is doing twice the work you are."

"I know, sarge. That's what I've been telling him for the last hour, but he won't slow down."

• • •

Teacher, to tardy student: "Why are you late?"

Barry: "Well, a sign down the street said — "

Teacher, interrupting: "Now what can a sign possibly have to do with it?"

Barry: "The sign said: 'School ahead; go slow.'"

SMELL

They that smell least, smell best.

• • •

Army
Recruit: "Sarge, I've got a pet skunk."

Sergeant: "Where do you expect to keep him."

Recruit: "Under my bunk in the barracks."

Sergeant: "What about the smell?"

Recruit: "He's gonna have to get used to it the same as I did."

• • •

"What's that peculiar odor I smell around this post office?"

"Probably the dead letters."

SMILE

If you see someone without a smile give him one of yours.

• • •

Wrinkles should merely indicate where smiles have been.

Mark Twain

• • •

Face value.

• • •

Smile on the world and it will smile on you; frown, and it will frown.

• • •

Talkative tourist to bus driver: "How will I know when to get off at my street?"

Driver: "Just watch for the big smile on my face."

●   ●   ●

The robb'd that smiles, steals something from the thief.

Shakespeare

SMOGARIAN

The city slicker was out to convince his country cousin that he was much smarter.

I'll prove it," he said. "I will give you a dollar for every question you ask that I can't answer, and you give me fifty cents for every one you can't."

It was agreed and the country boy allowed to ask the first question.

"What has seven legs, three green eyes, and lays eggs?" he asked the city cousin.

"I don't know," came the reply. "Here's the dollar I owe you. What is it?"

"I don't know either," replied the country cousin. "Here's the fifty cents I owe you."

●   ●   ●

Pa and Ma had worked hard all their lives to scratch out a meager living on their little farm up in the hills. When they reached age 65 they decided to retire and draw their Social Security.

Since they now had a steady income, they decided to take their entire life savings and buy the one thing they had always wanted — a new car. They purchased a new station wagon for $6,000. It was loaded with all the extras...even down to the beautiful metal on the sides that looked like wood.

When they got home, Pa got out the crowbar and proceeded to pry off the panels on the sides and back that looked like wood. When he was finished he stood back and surveyed his handiwork and said, "You know, Ma, I think I liked it better when it was in the crate."

●   ●   ●

A bomb fell on Italy and slid off.

●   ●   ●

A motorist, seeing a farmer hold a pig up to a tree while he gobbled apples, stopped in amazement. This was repeated several times and finally as the farmer's muscles bulged over a particularly heavy pig, the motorist walked over to the farmer.

"Excuse me," he said, "But isn't it an awful waste of time to feed pigs that way?"

The farmer held his pig closer to more apples, caught his breath and answered, "What is time to a pig?"

●   ●   ●

Billy: "How's your father coming with his new dairy farm?"

Silly: "Grand. He makes all the cows sleep on their backs."

Billy: "What's the idea?"

Silly: "So the cream will be on top in the morning."

●   ●   ●

A tobacco farmer was showing a visiting lady around his plantation.

"These are tobacco plants in full bloom," he explained.

"Isn't that wonderful!" she

gushed. "And when will the cigars be ripe?"

• • •

Visitor: "Why is your dog watching me so intently while I eat?"

Host: "Maybe it's because you are eating out of his plate."

• • •

Did you hear about the Smogarian who phoned the bank teller and said, "This is a stick-up; mail me ten thousand dollars."

• • •

Did you hear about the Smogarian inmates in a certain mental institution that became such expert divers that the superintendent decided to put water in the pool.

• • •

Did you hear about the Smogarian who tried to swim the English Channel...halfway across, he decided he couldn't make it so he swam back.

• • •

Smogarian: It took me twenty minutes to write a message to the milkman.

Man: Yes, I saw you. Next time why don't you write on the paper before you put it into the bottle?"

• • •

Man: Why don't you take your handkerchief all the way out of your pocket when you use it?

Smogarian: That ain't my handkerchief. That's my shirt tail.

• • •

Man: Why are you standing on your head?

Smogarian: Man, I've got a problem.

Man: What kind of problem?

Smogarian: I have no belt to hold up my pants.

• • •

Smogarian: I want two tickets for tonight's performance.

Box Office Man: We have no seats left...only two standing room left.

Smogarian: Are they together?

• • •

Smogarian: I was getting ten dollars a week and the boss just doubled my salary.

Man: What are you getting now?

Smogarian: Ten dollars every two weeks.

• • •

Did you hear about the two Smogarians who hired a woman to come in every week and dirty up?

• • •

Patient: I snore so loudly at night Doctor, that I wake myself up.

Doctor: I suggest you sleep in another room.

• • •

Jack: This tooth keeps me awake at night. What can I do for it?

Elmer: Maybe you should get a job as a night watchman.

SMOKE

Jay: Does the Bible say that if you smoke you can't get to heaven?

Bufe: No, but the more you smoke the quicker you'll get there.

SMOKING

The best way to stop smoking is

to carry wet matches.

• • •

Much smoking kills live men and cures dead swine.

SNORE
How come people who snore always fall asleep first?

SNOUT
A beautiful woman lacking discretion and modesty is like a fine gold ring in a pig's snout.

Proverbs 11:22

SNOW
Snow is the peanut butter of nature. It's crunchy, kids love it, and it clings to the roof of your house.

SOLOMON
Rich: Why was Solomon the wisest man in the world?

Dave: Because he had so many wives to advise him.

SOPRANO
Man is peculiar. He will torture animals but do nothing about a radio soprano or a singing commercial.

SORROW
Sorrow will pay no debt.

• • •

The thief is sorry he is to be hanged, not that he is a thief.

• • •

Sorrow seems to linger long.

• • •

Little griefs are loud, great sorrows are silent.

SOUP
It is better to eat soup with someone you love than steak with someone you hate. Proverbs 15:17

SOWING AND REAPING
Sow a thought, you reap an act
Sow an act, you reap a habit
Sow a habit, you reap a character
Sow a character, you reap a destiny.

SPACE
Boastful Soldier, at a party: "The bullet struck my head and went careening into space."

Bored Friend: "You're being honest about it, anyway."

SPANKING
Something that is inflicted on one end to impress the other.

• • •

Too many parents are not on spanking terms with their children.

SPEAK
"Did you ever hear me speak?"

"I never heard you do anything else."

SPEAKER
If a speaker rehearses his speeches, can you say that he practices what he preaches?

SPEAKING
A speechmaker's closing remark: "I have a lot more to say but I try to observe the first rule of public speaking: Nice guys finish fast!"

• • •

Want of study, and want of really knowing what one is driving at, must bear the blame of many a long and weary talk. Hence a short speech is usually of better quality than a long one; and if it is not, it is all the better that it is short.

SPECIALIST
A doctor with a smaller practice but a bigger yacht.

SPECTATOR

A baseball fan is a spectator sitting 400 feet from the plate who can see better than an umpire standing five feet away.

SPEECH

How great a matter a little fire kindleth!

• • •

The man of few words and settled mind is wise; therefore, even a fool is thought to be wise when he is silent. It pays him to keep his mouth shut.

Proverbs 17:27-28

• • •

The many quips from Sir Winston Churchill are legendary. One of our favorites is when he was asked, ''Doesn't it thrill you to know that everytime you make a speech the hall is packed to overflowing?''

''It is quite flattering,'' Sir Winston replied. ''But whenever I feel that way I always remember that, if instead of making a political speech, I was being hanged, the crowd would be twice as big.''

• • •

Blessed are they who have nothing to say and who cannot be persuaded to say it.

• • •

The mouth of the wise man is like a money box which is seldom opened.

• • •

Self-control means controlling the tongue! A quick retort can ruin everything.   Proverbs 13:3

• • •

The true use of speech is not so much to express our wants as to conceal them.   Oliver Goldsmith

• • •

Half the world is composed of people who have something to say and can't, and the other half who have nothing to say and keep on saying it.   Robert Frost

• • •

It usually takes more than three weeks to prepare a good impromptu speech.   Mark Twain

• • •

A man may dig his grave with his teeth.

• • •

Keep your mouth closed and you'll stay out of trouble.

Proverbs 21:23

• • •

It used to take a miracle to make an ass speak; now it requires a miracle to prevent them from speaking.

• • •

Flies don't enter a closed mouth.

• • •

When in doubt what to say, say nothing.   La Rochefoucauld

• • •

A good man thinks before he speaks; the evil man pours out his evil words without a thought.

Proverbs 15:28

• • •

Be patient and you will finally win, for a soft tongue can break hard bones.   Proverbs 25:15

• • •

Some people like to make

cutting remarks, but the words of the wise soothe and heal.

Proverbs 12:18

● ● ●

Be silent or say something better than silence. Pythagoras

● ● ●

Great talkers are like leaky pitchers, everything runs out.

● ● ●

It is better to be silent and be thought a fool than to speak up and remove all doubt.

● ● ●

To quarrel with a neighbor is foolish; a man with good sense holds his tongue. Proverbs 11:12

● ● ●

Keep your mouth shut, and no flies will get in.

SPEEDING

Motorist stopped by traffic officer: "I was temporarily overcome by a wave of nostalgia. I thought the speed limit was 70."

● ● ●

Anybody who doesn't cut his speed at the sight of a police car is probably parked.

● ● ●

Policeman: You were going over sixty.

Motorist: Imagine that! A twenty - mile - an - hour tail wind.

SPELLING

Mother: My child is a genius. He has so many original ideas hasn't he?

Teacher: Yes, especially when it comes to spelling.

SPHINX

Professor: "Jones, can you tell me who built the Sphinx?"

Student: "I-I-I did know, sir, but I've forgotten."

Professor: "Great guns, what a calamity! The only man living who knows, and he has forgotten!"

SPINSTER

Lady in waiting.

SPLINTERS

Chet: How did you get your hand full of splinters?

Jack: I was out hunting...and caught a timber wolf bare-handed.

SPOILED

Many a good tale is spoiled in the telling.

SPOKESMAN

He who talks like a big wheel may be only a spokesman.

SPONSOR

News announcer:

"Bulletin! Russia has just invaded the United States...but first, a word from our sponsor.

SPORT CARS

One nice thing about small sport cars...if you flood the carburetor, you can just put the car over your shoulder and burp it.

SPRING CLEANING

Rearranging the dust.

SPRINGTIME

On the first day of springtime my true love gave to me: five packs of seed, four sacks of fertilizer, three cans of weed killer, two bottles of insect spray, and a pruning knife for the pear tree.

STALK
Baby ear of corn: "Mamma, where did I come from?

Momma ear of corn: "Hush, darling, the stalk brought you."

STARS
The stars make no noise.

STARTING
The journey of a thousand miles begins with one pace.

STATION
A janitor who worked in a railroad station decided to get married in a huge room on the upper floor of the station. So many friends and kinfolk showed up, their combined weight caused the building to collapse. Moral of the story: Never marry above your station.

STATISTICS
Can be used to prove almost anything...even truth.

• • •

A professor of statistics, about to retire, bought himself a tiny island — then christened it "Percent Isle."

STEADY
Bill: "I'm a steady worker."
Bob: "Yeah, and if you were any steadier, you would be motionless."

STEAL
Who steals a pin will steal a greater thing.

• • •

Do not move the ancient boundary marks. That is stealing.
Proverbs 22:28

STEAM
Too many people work up a

head of steam before they find out what's cooking.

STOMACH
The way to a man's heart is through his stomach, but who wants to go through his stomach?

STONE
"My husband didn't leave a bit of insurance."

"Then where did you get that gorgeous diamond ring?"

"Well, he left $1,000 for his casket and $5,000 for a stone. This is the stone."

STOOPING
If some people live up to their ideas they would be stooping.

STORY
We like the fellow who says he is going to make a long story short, and does.

STORYTELLER
A good storyteller is a person who has a good memory and hopes other people haven't.

STRANGERS
Be not forgetful to entertain strangers: for thereby some have entertained angels unawares.
Hebrews 13:2, KJV

STRENGTH
The glory of young men is their strength; of old men, their experience.
Proverbs 20:29

STRIFE
If you want to avoid domestic strife, don't marry in January...and that goes for the other months, too.

• • •

A dry crust eaten in peace is better than steak everyday along

with argument and strife.
Proverbs 17:1

STRIKE

Not only strike while the iron is hot, but make it hot by striking.
Cromwell

•   •   •

John: There's talk that the men are going out on strike.

Tim: What for?

John: Shorter hours.

Tim: That's good. I always did think that sixty minutes is too long for an hour.

STUDY

The more we study the more we discover our ignorance.

STUFFED SHIRT

A stuffed shirt is usually all front.

STUPID

Are you naturally stupid or did a Cuban hijack your brain?

SUBMISSION

If two people ride the same horse, one must ride behind.

SUCCESS

To climb steep hills requires slow pace at first.
William Shakespeare

•   •   •

The success of the wicked entices many more.

•   •   •

Nothing recedes like success.
Walter Winchell

•   •   •

Success comes in cans; failure in can'ts.

•   •   •

Don't just envy another's good fortune; emulate the work that helped earn it.

•   •   •

The dictionary is the only place where success comes before work.

•   •   •

If at first you don't succeed, try a little ardor.

SUE

A first grader slipped in the hall of the school and sprained his ankle. His teacher, hurrying to console him said, "Remember, Johnny, big boys don't cry."

"I'm not going to cry," snapped Johnny. "I'm going to sue."

SUFFER

Great souls suffer in silence.

•   •   •

Some persons won't suffer in silence because that would take the pleasure out of it.

SUFFICIENT

A word to the wife is rarely sufficient.

SUGAR

Ben: "One of our little pigs was sick so I gave him some sugar."

Dan: "Sugar! What for?"

Ben: "Haven't you ever heard of sugar-cured ham?"

SUGGESTIONS

Friendly suggestions are as pleasant as perfume.   Proverbs 27:9

SUICIDE

The last thing a person should do.

SUIT

I have a suit for every day of the year...the one I'm wearing.

SULTAN

Sultan to small boy: "Go ask one of your mothers."

SUNBURN

I fell asleep on the beach and burned my stomach. You should see my pot roast!

• • •

If you want a place in the sun, you've got to expect a little sunburn.

SUNDAY SCHOOL

The road to success is dotted with many tempting parking places.

• • •

Son: Dad, did you go to Sunday School when you were young?
Dad: Never missed a Sunday.
Son: Bet it won't do me any good either.

SUNSHINE

All sunshine makes the desert.

SUPERIORITY

My kid sister has a superiority complex...she thinks she's almost as good as me.

SUPERSTAR

Joe: Did you see the show JESUS CHRIST, SUPER-STAR?
What did you think of it?
Moe: It's not as good as the Book!

SURLY

Cheerful people, the doctors say,resist disease better than the glum ones. In other words, the surly bird catches the germ.

SURPRISE

Faint praise ne'er won fair lady, but it would certainly surprise many wives.

• • •

I was so surprised at my birth, I couldn't speak for a year and a half.

• • •

"My fiance's birthday is next week and I want to give him a surprise. What would you suggest?"

"Tell him your real age!"

• • •

There was a farmer whose wife was always after him to replace his ancient, tattered working clothes. One day he drove to town to sell some vegetables and he found himself with a few more dollars than he had expected to make from the sale. Remembering his wife's pleas, he bought himself a new set of clothing and leaving the bundle under the seat of his pickup truck he went off to do a few more errands. Then he started to drive home. On the way, thinking of the bundle of new clothing, he said to himself "Why not give the old lady a surprise." He stopped his truck beside a swift-flowing river, got out, took off all of the old clothes he was wearing and threw them into the river. He stood and watched them drift downstream and vanish from sight. Then he reached into the truck for the bundle of new clothes. The bundle was gone. Somebody had stolen it. The farmer considered the situation for a moment then climbed back into the truck, shrugging his bare shoulders philosophically, he continued on home.

"Well," he said. "We'll still give the old lady a surprise!"

●   ●   ●

I love surprises — as long as I'm ready for them.

SURRENDER
Another word for engagement.

SUSPICION
The less we know the more we suspect.   Josh Billings

SWAP
Seems that a tribal chieftain's daughter was offered as a bride to the son of a neighboring potentate in exchange for two cows and four sheep. The big swap was to be effected on the shore of the stream that separated the two tribes. Pop and his daughter showed up at the appointed time only to discover that the groom and his livestock were on the other side of the stream. The father grunted, "The fool doesn't know which side his bride is bartered on."

SWEATER
A garment worn by a child when his mother feels chilly.

SWEEP
A new broom sweeps well, but an old one is best for the corners.

SWELL
"I can't get into my shoes."
"What is the matter...did your feet swell too?"

SWELL-HEAD
Nature's frantic effort to fill a vacuum.

SYNONYM
Mother (helping small son with his language lesson): "What is a synonym?"

Small Son (smacking lips in pleasant memories): "Synonym is something you put in rolls."

TACT
Tact is the ability to close one's mouth before someone else wants to do it.

●   ●   ●

Social lying.

TALEBEARER
A talehearer is brother to a talebearer.

TALK
Talk is cheap because the supply is greater than the demand.

●   ●   ●

Those who love to talk will suffer the consequences. Men have died for saying the wrong thing.
           Proverbs 18:21

●   ●   ●

Some people have the gift of compressing the largest amount of words into the smallest amount of thought.   Winston Churchill

●   ●   ●

Why do we all want to talk about ourselves when that's the subject we know least about.

●   ●   ●

One may say too much even upon the best subject.

TALKER
A great talker may be no fool, but he is one that relies on him.

●   ●   ●

Two great talkers will not travel far together.

TALKING

Long talking begets short hearing.

* * *

The other day I was driving under the influence of my wife. She talks and talks and talks. She gets two thousand words to the gallon.

* * *

Son: What do you call it when one woman is talking?
Dad: Monologue.
Son: What do you call it when two women are talking?
Dad: Cat-alogue.

* * *

Young Tom told his father that when he grew up, he wanted to drive a big army tank.

"Well, Son," said his dad, "if that's what you want to do, I certainly won't stand in your way."

TANTRUM

A bicycle built for two.

TASKS

Some tasks have to be put off dozens of times before they will completely slip your mind.

TASTES

He who tastes every man's broth sometimes burns his mouth.

TAX

The income tax has made more liars out of the American people than gold has.   Will Rogers

* * *

What is the difference between a taxidermist and a tax collector?

The taxidermist takes only your skin.   Mark Twain

* * *

The tax collector must love poor people — he's creating so many of them.

* * *

Nothing makes time pass more quickly than an income tax installment every three months.

TAX ASSESSOR

The only one who shows a sincere appreciation of your efforts to improve your home is the tax assessor.

TAX COLLECTOR

The difference between a tax collector and a taxidermist is that the taxidermist leaves the hide intact.

TAXES

The reward for saving your money is being able to pay your taxes without borrowing.

* * *

An American can consider himself a success when it costs him more to support the government than to support a wife and children.

* * *

It's awfully difficult to believe that only about 200 years ago we went to war to avoid taxation.

* * *

I'm gonna put all my money into taxes. They're sure to go up.

* * *

Income Tax Song: "Everything I have is yours."

* * *

April 15 should be called Tax-giving day.

● ● ●

Taxpayer:	I always pay my income tax all at once.
Tax Collector:	But you are allowed to pay it in quarterly installments.
Taxpayer:	I know it, but my heart can't stand it four times a year.

TAXPAYER

Taxpayers: People who don't have to pass civil service examinations in order to work for the government.

● ● ●

What this country needs is some social workers to look after broken down taxpayers.

TEA

Three Englishmen stopped at a restaurant for a spot of tea. The waiter appeared with pad and pencil.

"I'll have a glass of weak tea," ordered the first.

"I'll have tea, too," said the second, "but very strong with two pieces of lemon."

"Tea for me, too, please," said the third. "But be sure the glass is absolutely clean."

In a short time the waiter was back with the order. "All right," he asked. "Which one gets the clean glass?"

TEACHER

Teacher: "A fool can ask more questions than a wise man can answer."

Student: "No wonder so many of us flunk our exams."

● ● ●

A wise teacher makes learning a joy; a rebellious teacher spouts foolishness.   Proverbs 15:2

● ● ●

The best teacher — one who makes you want to learn.

● ● ●

Abraham Lincoln told this story of Daniel Webster's boyhood:

Young Daniel was not noted for tidiness. One day in the district school the teacher told him if he appeared in school again with such dirty hands, she would thrash him. But the next day Daniel appeared with his hands in the same condition.

"Daniel," the teacher said in desperation, "hold out your hand!"

Daniel spat on his palm, rubbed it on the seat of his trousers, and held it out. The teacher surveyed it in disgust. "Daniel," she exclaimed, "if you can find me a hand in this school that is dirtier than this one here, I will let you off."

Daniel promptly held out his other hand. The teacher had to keep her word.

TEARS

The most efficient water power in the world — women's tears.

TEENAGERS

"What did your teenage daughter do all summer?"

"Her hair and her nails!"

● ● ●

Oh, to be only half as wonderful as my child thought I was. And only half as stupid as my teenager thinks I am.

• • •

Father to teenage daughter: ''I want you home by 11 o'clock.''

''But Daddy, I'm no longer a child.''

''I know, that's why I want you home by 11.''

• • •

A teenager is someone who can eat his heart out without affecting his appetite.

• • •

Dialogue between teenager and parent:

''I'm off to the party.''

''Well, have a good time.''

''Look, Pop, don't tell me what to do.''

• • •

If you live in a house full of teenagers, it is not necessary to ask for whom the bell tolls. It's not for you.

• • •

Dad: Did you use the car last night?

Son: Yes, Dad. I took some of the boys for a ride.

Dad: Well, tell them I found two of their lipsticks.

• • •

About the time the bedtime stories are televised, many youngsters are going out for the evening.

TEETH

There are three basic rules for having good teeth:

1. Brush them twice a day.
2. See your dentist twice a year.

3. Keep your nose out of other people's business.

• • •

Teeth placed before the tongue give good advice.

TELEPHONE

Mother: Is this telephone call really necessary?

Daughter: How can I tell till I've made it?

• • •

Did you hear about the teenager who plans to run away from home just as soon as she gets a long enough telephone extension cord?

TELEVISION

Television is now so desperately hungry for material that they're scraping the top of the barrel.

Gore Vidal

• • •

Know what TV is? The place where little old movies go when they're bad.

• • •

New TV shows are so bad this season the kids are doing their homework again.

• • •

The characters on those TV soap operas never watch TV soap operas.

• • •

You can never hope to become a skilled conversationalist until you learn how to put your foot tactfully through the television set.

• • •

There is talk that the next war will be fought with the television. I'm in training. I've faced some terrible programs.

• • •

The trouble with TV is that we sit so much watching the 21-inch screen we develop a 50-inch bottom.

•   •   •

Early to bed and early to rise is a sure sign that you don't care for television.

•   •   •

Television hero — one who sits through the program.

TEMPER

There is more hope for a fool than for a man of quick temper.

Proverbs 29:20

•   •   •

Something you never loose, because it is always there when you need it.

•   •   •

The worst-tempered people I've ever met were people who knew they were wrong.

•   •   •

A tart temper never mellows with age; and a sharp tongue is the only edged tool that grows keener with constant use.

Washington Irving

•   •   •

Men lose their tempers in defending their taste.

Ralph Waldo Emerson

•   •   •

Keep your temper; no one else wants it.

•   •   •

A wise man controls his temper. He knows that anger causes mistakes.   Proverbs 14:29

•   •   •

A quick-tempered man starts fights; a cool-tempered man tries to stop them.   Proverbs 15:18

TEMPTATION

When you flee temptation, be sure you don't leave a forwarding address.

•   •   •

There are several good protections against temptation, but the surest is cowardice.   Mark Twain

•   •   •

No man knows how bad he is until he has tried to be good. There is a silly idea about that good people don't know what temptation means.   C. S. Lewis: The Screwtape Letters

•   •   •

Do we ever have a temptation without previous preparation?

•   •   •

Some temptations come to the industrious, but all temptations attack the idle.

Charles Haddon Spurgeon

TENDER

Question: Why did the locomotive refuse to sit?

Answer: Because it had a tender behind.

TERMINAL

It's all right to have a train of thoughts, if you have a terminal.

TERMITE

Did you hear about the termite with false teeth? He walked into a tavern and asked respectfully, "Is the bar tender here?"

•   •   •

Did you hear about the hungry termite that got relief from a welfare board?

•   •   •

...newly hatched termites are babes in the wood.

TEST

The test: Could I? Would I? Should I? and Will I?

TEXAN

A Texas rancher was visiting an Iowa farm. The Iowa farmer was justly proud of his 200 acres of rich, productive land.

"Is this your whole farm?" the Texan asked. "Why back in Texas I get in my car at 5:00 in the morning, and I drive and drive all day. At dusk I just reach the other end of my ranch."

The Iowa farmer thought a while and replied, "I used to have a car like that."

• • •

Did you hear about the Texan whose bankroll was so big he had to put it on microfilm before he could put it in his pocket.

THEOLOGY

Division has done more to hide Christ from the view of all men than all the infidelity that has ever been spoken.

THEORY

I never once made a discovery...I speak without exaggeration that I have constructed three thousand different theories in connection with the electric light...yet in only two cases did my experiments prove the truth of my theory.

Thomas A. Edison

• • •

There can be no theory of any account unless it corroborate with the theory of the earth.

Walt Whitman

THINK

The less a man thinks, the more he talks.

• • •

The reason some of us find it difficult to think is that we haven't had any previous experience.

• • •

There are two kinds of thinkers in the world. Those who think they can and those who think they can't...and they're both right.

• • •

The person who thinks before he speaks is silent most of the time.

THIRTY

A nice age for a woman, especially if she happens to be forty.

THOUGHT

You are today what you thought yesterday.

• • •

The main reason that some of us get lost in thought is that it is such unfamiliar territory.

THOUGHTFUL

He was the kind of thoughtful person who never forgot himself.

THREATEN

Who threatens most is he who most doth fear.

When a youth begins to sow wild oats, it's time for father to start the threshing machine.

THUMB

"Waiter," exclaimed the angry diner, "You've got your thumb on my steak!"

"I'm sorry, sir," the waiter replied, "But I didn't want it to fall on the floor again."

• • •

A man with a green thumb is a good gardener, but a man with a purple thumb is a nearsighted carpenter.

TIGER

He who rides a tiger is afraid to dismount.

TIGHT

He's so tight he keeps five dollar bills folded so long, Lincoln gets ingrown whiskers.

TIME

Lost, yesterday, somewhere between sunrise and sunset, two golden hours, each set with sixty diamond minutes. No reward is offered for they are gone forever.
                              Horace Mann

• • •

Time and tide wait for no man, but time always stands still for a woman of 30.   Robert Frost

• • •

Time may be a great healer, but it's a lousy beautician.

• • •

Why is it that there is never enough time to do it right, but there is always enough time to do it over!   Mark Twain

• • •

People who have half an hour to spend usually spend it with someone who hasn't.

• • •

Time is what passes between pay days.

• • •

Maybe people who are always on time aren't doing it to be courteous and polite. Maybe they're just mean, vicious people whose ambition in life is to make the rest of us feel guilty for being late.

• • •

1st boy: I wonder what time it is?

2nd boy: It can't be four o'clock yet, because my mother said I was to be home at four, and I'm not.

• • •

They who make the worst use of their time most complain of its shortness.

TIP

Did you ever stop to think that the tip you leave for a meal today would have paid the whole bill ten years ago.

• • •

If you can't get away for a vacation, just tip every third person you meet and you'll get the same effect.

TITLE

In an age when everyone seems to be playing the name game of glorifying job titles, the man in charge of the meat department at a store in Wichita Falls, Texas, deserves a round of applause. On his weekly time card he describes his position as "Meat Head."

TOBACCO

A nauseating plant consumed by only two creatures: a large green worm and man; the worm doesn't know any better.

TOE

Nothing is harder to do secretly than stub your toe.

TOLERANCE

Broad-minded is just another way of saying a fellow's too lazy to form an opinion.   Will Rogers

TOM

"My name is T-t-t-t-tom."

"I'll call you Tom for short."

TOMORROW

For yesterday is but a dream and tomorrow is only a vision but today well lived makes yesterday a dream of happiness and every tomorrow a vision of hope.

•   •   •

"To-morrow" — the day on which idle men work.

TONGUE

The tongue the ambassador of the heart.

•   •   •

Hold your tongue, and hold your friend.

•   •   •

The tongue is in a wet place, and easily slips.

•   •   •

A sharp tongue is the only edge tool that grows keener with constant use.   Washington Irving

•   •   •

Many have fallen by the edge of the sword; but not so many as have fallen by the tongue.

•   •   •

Don't let your tongue say what your head may pay for.

TONGUE TWISTER

According to the **Guinness Book of Records**, the toughest tongue-twister in the English language is this one: "The sixth sick sheik's sixth sheep's sick."

TOOTHACHE

There was never yet philosopher
That could endure the toothache patiently.   Shakespeare

TOP THIS

Bill: My dog swallowed a tape worm and died by inches.

Bob: That's nothing, my dog crawled in on my bed and died by the foot.

Ken: I can beat that. I had a dog that went out of the house and died by the yard.

TOTAL

The sum total of our national debt is some total.

TOUPEE

"How do you like my new toupee?"

"Marvelous...you can't tell it from a wig."

TOURIST

A person who travels 1,000 miles to get a picture of himself standing by his car.

TRAIN

Many people seem to think America has only one train (the gravy train). On it they insist on being the conductor.

•   •   •

"Did you miss that train, sir?"

"No! I didn't like the looks of it, so I chased it out of the station."

TRAIN OF THOUGHT

"Be quiet. You're interrupting my train of thought."

"Let me know when it comes to a station."

TRAMP

A tramp knocked at a door and asked the lady for something to eat. "Yes, I'll give you something to eat if you chop the wood and hoe the garden first."

"Lady," replied the tramp, "I asked for a donation, not a transaction."

TRAP

The man who sets a trap for others will get caught in it himself. Roll a boulder down on someone, and it will roll back and crush you.
Proverbs 26:27

TRAVEL

In America there are two classes of travel — first class, and with children.   Robert Benchley

● ● ●

The world is a book, and those who do not travel, read only a page.   St. Augustine

● ● ●

Question: What broadens people and also flattens them at the same time?
Answer: Travel.

TREADS

There was once a wise man who loved a beautiful maiden, but she lived in a marsh where his car always got stuck and besides, her father had a gun, so he never did get close enough to tell her of his passion. However, she had a more energetic suitor who purchased amphibious tires for his car and, when her father was asleep, speedily carried her off.

Moral: Treads rush in where wise men fear to fool.

TRIALS

A gem cannot be polished without friction, nor a man perfected without trials.

TRIFLES

Small ills are the fountains of most of our groans.

Men trip not on mountains, they stumble on stones.

● ● ●

A small leak will sink a great ship.   Benjamin Franklin

● ● ●

For the want of a nail the shoe was lost,
For the want of a shoe the horse was lost,
For the want of a horse the rider was lost,
For the want of a rider the battle was lost,
For the want of a battle the kingdom was lost,
And all for the want of a horseshoe nail. Benjamin Franklin

● ● ●

It is the little bits of things that fret and worry us; we can dodge an elephant, but we can't dodge a fly.
Josh Billings

TRIUMPH

Triumph is just "umph" added to "try."

TROUBLE

The easiest thing in the world to borrow.

● ● ●

The only fellow whose troubles are all behind him is a school bus driver.

● ● ●

The darkest hour has but sixty minutes.

A misty morning does not signify a cloudy day.

• • •

Supply Officer: "Does the new uniform fit you?"

Recruit: "The jacket isn't bad, sir, but the trousers are a little loose around the armpits."

TRUST

Trust in your money and down you go! Trust in God and flourish as a tree!   Proverbs 11:28

• • •

In God we trust — all others pay cash.

• • •

Don't pick me up before I fall down.

TRUSTED

To be trusted is a greater compliment than to be loved.

TRUSTWORTHY

A servant is known by his master's absence.

TRUTH

Craft must have clothes, but truth loves to go naked.

Thomas Fuller

• • •

Truth gets well if she is run over by a locomotive, while Error dies of lockjaw if she scratches her finger.

William Cullen Bryant

• • •

The greatest homage we can pay to truth, is to use it.

James Russell Lowell

• • •

Truth has only to change hands a few times to become fiction.

• • •

Truth stands the test of time; lies are soon exposed.

Proverbs 12:19

• • •

Any story sounds true until someone tells the other side and sets the record straight.

Proverbs 18:17

• • •

Error always rides the back of truth.

• • •

Follow truth too close at the heels and 'twill kick out your teeth.

• • •

Truth sits upon the lips of dying men.   Andrew Arnold

• • •

Truth needs not many words, but a false tale, a large preamble.

• • •

My way of joking is to tell the truth. It's the funniest joke in the world.   G. B. Shaw

TRUTHFULNESS

There's no limit to the height a man can attain by remaining on the level.

TRYING

Mother: "Johnny, this isn't a very good report card. Are you trying."

Johnny: "Yes, my teacher said I am the most trying boy in the class."

• • •

Mother, having finally tucked a small boy into bed after an unusually trying day: "Well, I've worked today from son-up to son-down!"

TWINS

Melba: I guess your husband was pleased when he found himself the father of twin boys.

Pam: Was he! He went around grinning from heir to heir.

● ● ●

Insult added to injury.

UNAWARE

Question: What is the meaning of the word "unaware"?

Answer: Unaware is what you put on first and take off last.

UNBALANCED

They say that one in every four Americans is unbalanced. Think of your three closest friends. If they seem OK, then you're in trouble.

UNDERSTANDING

He who does not understand your silence will probably not understand your words.

UNDERTAKER

The last man to let you down.

● ● ●

Dave: Did you hear about the snake charmer who married an undertaker?

Rich: No, what happened?

Dave: They had towels marked "Hiss" and "Hearse."

UNDERWEAR

Something that creeps up on you.

UNEARTHLY

Mother: Did the music teacher really say your voice was heavenly?

Son: Well, sort of — she said it was unearthly.

UNION

Man filling out an application for union membership: "Does this union have any death benefits?"

"Sure does," replied the union representative. "When you die you don't have to pay any more dues."

UNITY

A house divided against itself cannot stand. Jesus

UNIVERSITY

Universities are full of knowledge; the freshmen bring a little in and the seniors take none away, and knowledge accumulates.

UNKEMPT

A guy goes to the doctor and the doctor says, "You have the dirtiest, most unkempt, uncivilized body I have ever seen." The patient says, "That's funny, that's what the other doctor told me yesterday." "Then why did you come to see me?" The patient answers, "I wanted a second opinion."

UNKNOWN

It is dangerous and sinful to rush into the unknown. Proverbs 19:2

UNRELIABLE

An unreliable messenger can cause a lot of trouble. Reliable communication permits progress.
Proverbs 13:17

● ● ●

Putting confidence in an unreliable man is like chewing with a sore tooth, or trying to run on a broken foot. Proverbs 25:19

UNWIND

You never know what makes some people tick until they begin to unwind.

VACATION

A period of travel and relaxation when you take twice the clothes and half the money you need.

• • •

No man needs a vacation so much as the man who has just had one.

• • •

A vacation resort is where you go when you are worn out and where you come back from a complete wreck.

• • •

The bigger the summer vacation the harder the fall.

VACUUM CLEANER

Mother: Glen, the canary has disappeared.

Glen: That's funny. It was there just now when I tried to clean the cage with the vacuum cleaner.

VALUE

If a man empties his purse into his head, no one can take it from him.   Franklin

VARIETY

With me a change of trouble is as good as a vacation.

William Lloyd George

VASE

Benjie: "Mom, do you remember that vase you always worried I would break?

Mom: "Yes, what about it?"

Benjie: "Your worries are over."

VEGETABLES

A vegetable is a substance used to balance a child's plate while it's being carried to and from the table.

• • •

Hostess to dinner guests: "All the vegetables are from our garden — you're eating a $100-a-plate dinner."

VENGEANCE

Deep vengeance is the daughter of deep silence.

• • •

Avenge not yourselves, but rather give place unto wrath: for it is written, Vengeance is mine; I will repay, saith the Lord.

Romans 12:19, KJV

VENTURE

Mother to small boy about to venture into a crowd on his own: "Remember, if you get lost, come right back here!"

VERBOSITY

Inebriated with the exuberance of his own verbosity.

Benjamin Disraeli

VICE

Wild oats make a bad autumn crop.

• • •

Our pleasant vices

Are made the whip to scourge us.   Shakespeare

VICTORY

Go ahead and prepare for the conflict, but victory comes from God.   Proverbs 21:31

• • •

A good general not only sees the way to victory; he also knows when victory is impossible.

VIEW
You must scale the mountain if you would view the plain.

VIOLENCE
Nothing good ever comes of violence.   Martin Luther

VISE
Linda: What's that you have there?

Jack: A clamp.

Linda: Oh, so you're a vise guy.

VISION
One may have good eyes, and see nothing.

•   •   •

Don't call the world dirty because you have forgotten to clean your glasses.

VISITORS
Why are trees in winter like troublesome visitors?

Because it's a long time before they leave.

•   •   •

Fish and visitors smell in three days.

VOICE
Pretty Young Student: "Professor Boschovich, do you think I will ever be able to do anything with my voice?"

Weary Teacher: "Well it might come in handy in case of fire or shipwreck."

VOLKSWAGEN
They're calling Volkswagen's new Rabbit "Bug's Bunny."

VOMIT
As a dog returns to his vomit, so a fool repeats his folly.
                Proverbs 26:11

VOW
Vows made in storms are forgotten in calm.   Thomas Fuller

WAITER
Diner: Is it customary to tip the waiter in this restaurant?

Waiter: Why...ah...yes, sir.

Diner: Then hand me a tip. I've waited almost an hour for that steak I ordered.

•   •   •

A waiter is one that believes that money grows on trays.

WALLPAPERING
Wallpapering is easy once you get the hang of it.

WAR
Another thing against war is that it seldom if ever kills off the right people.

WASHINGTON
Washington, D.C.: Fund city.

WASTEBASKET
Next to automation nothing beats a wastebasket for speeding up work.

WATERMELONS
Fruit and vegetable market: "Best watermelons you ever seed."

•   •   •

Two watermelons cannot be held under one arm.

WEAKNESS
Don't judge your wife too

harshly for her weaknesses. If she didn't have them, chances are she would never have married you.

WEALTH

Is a curse when the neighbors have it.

•　　•　　•

A man is never so on trial as in the moment of good fortune.

Lew Wallace

•　　•　　•

Let me see your man dead and I will tell you how rich he is.

•　　•　　•

God shows His contempt for wealth by the kind of persons He selects to receive it.

WEATHER

Don't knock the weather; nine-tenths of the people couldn't start a conversation if it didn't change once in a while.

•　　•　　•

Everybody talks about the weather but nobody does anything about it.

•　　•　　•

Probably the last completely accurate weather forecast was when God told Noah there was a 100 percent chance of precipitation.

WEDDING

Where the bride looks stunning and the groom looks stunned.

•　　•　　•

From an engagement announcement in the Scranton, Pa., **Scrantonian**: "No fate has been set for the wedding."

•　　•　　•

A little girl at her first church wedding suddenly whispered loudly to her mother: "Mummy, has the lady changed her mind?"

"Why, dear, whatever do you mean?" her mother asked.

"Well, Mummy, she went up the aisle with one man and came back with another!"

•　　•　　•

Daddy was showing Junior the family album and came across the picture of himself and his wife on their wedding day.

"Was that the day Mom came to work for us?" Junior inquired.

•　　•　　•

A wedding is a funeral where you smell your own flowers.

•　　•　　•

Don: Do you think it's unlucky to postpone a wedding?

Rich: Not if you keep on doing it.

WEDLOCK

The chain of wedlock is so heavy that it takes two to carry it — sometimes three.　　Dumas

WEEDS

The best way to distinguish between weeds and flowers is to cut them all down; those that come up again are weeds.

•　　•　　•

There's no garden without weeds.

WEEVILS

Two boll weevils came from the country to the city. One became rich and famous. The other remained the lesser of the two weevils.

WEIGH

An Arab stood on a weighing machine in the light of the lingering day.

A counterfeit penny he dropped in the slot and silently stole a weigh.

WEIGHT

Some women would be more spic if they had less span.

WHALE

If fish is brain food, you had better eat a whale.

WHISPER

Some folks will believe anything if you whisper it.

• • •

Mother: What did you learn in school today?
Son: How to whisper without moving my lips.

WHISTLED

The biggest adjustment a bride must make is getting used to being whistled for instead of at.

WHISTLER'S MOTHER

A 12-year-old boy, temporarily dismissed from school for whistling in class, brought this note of apology from home: "Dear Miss M — Peter says that he is sorry that he whistled in your class and promises not to do so again." It was signed: "Whistler's Mother."

H. L. Reinhard, Jr.

WHITE HOUSE

Honorable mansion.

WICKED

The wicked enjoy fellowship with others who are wicked; liars enjoy liars.   Proverbs 17:4

WICKEDNESS

God bears with the wicked, but not forever.   Miguel de Cervantes

• • •

If men are so wicked with religion, what would they be without it?   Franklin

• • •

Wickedness loves company — and leads others into sin.

Proverbs 16:29

WIFE

A continual buzzing in a man's ear.

• • •

The man who finds a wife finds a good thing; she is a blessing to him from the Lord. Proverbs 18:22

• • •

Why a man wants a wife is a mystery. Why man wants two wives is a bigamistery.

• • •

Wife: "My husband and I like the same things — but it took him 16 years to learn."

• • •

A worthy wife is her husband's joy and crown; the other kind corrodes his strength and tears down everything he does.

Proverbs 12:4

• • •

One should choose a wife with his ears, rather than with his eyes.

• • •

An obedient wife commands her husband.

• • •

Joe: My uncle invented a machine where you put in a nickel and get a new wife.
Moe: Why doesn't he invent a

machine where you put in a wife and get a new nickel?

• • •

Rod: So your wife is very broad-minded?

Ron: Yes, she believes there are always two sides to an argument — hers and her mother's.

• • •

Rich: Have you ever suspected your wife of leading a double life?

Glen: Continually...her own and mine.

• • •

Some wives leave their husbands and take everything; others take everything, but don't leave.

• • •

"My wife kisses me only when she needs money."

"Don't you think that's often enough?"

• • •

Elmer: Does your wife pick your clothes?

Jack: No...just the pockets.

• • •

My wife and I always think exactly alike, only she usually has first think.

• • •

The sweetest thing in life
Is the welcome of a wife.

WIVES

Men do not know their wives well; but wives know their husbands perfectly.

WIG

A woman bought a new wig and thought it would be fun to surprise her husband at the office. She walked in and asked him, "Do you think you could find a place in your life for a person like me?"

"Not a chance," he snapped. "You remind me too much of my wife."

WILL

Lawyer, reading a wise old man's will to the relatives. "And being of sound mind, I spent every dollar I had."

• • •

A rich uncle died and a line in his will read as follows: "I leave to my beloved nephew all the money he owes me."

WILLING

A willing soldier will soon find a sword.

WILL POWER

Will power is not telling anybody you've quit smoking.

WIND

No wind is a good wind if you don't know where the harbor is.

• • •

A tourist traveling through Western Kansas saw a man sitting by the ruins of a house that had been blown away.

"Was this your house, my friend?" he asked sympathetically.

"Yep."

"Any of your family blown away with the house?"

"Yep, wife and four kids."

"Great Scott, man, why aren't you hunting for them?"

"Well, stranger, I've been in this country quite a spell. The wind's due to change this afternoon. So I figure I might as well wait here till it brings 'em back.''

WINE
When wine enters the head the secrets fly out.

WINE-AGE
People are like wine — age sours the bad and improves the good.

WISDOM
The older I grow the more I distrust the familiar doctrine that age brings wisdom.

• • •

A wise youth accepts his father's rebuke; a young mocker doesn't.
Proverbs 13:1

• • •

A wise man doesn't display his knowledge, but a fool displays his foolishness.   Proverbs 12:23

• • •

How much better is wisdom than gold, and understanding than silver!   Proverbs 16:16

• • •

The wise man saves for the future, but the foolish man spends whatever he gets.   Proverbs 21:20

• • •

He that gets money before he gets wit,
Will be but a short while master of it.

• • •

A wise man is mightier than a strong man. Wisdom is mightier than strength.   Proverbs 24:5

• • •

The fear of the Lord is the beginning of wisdom.
Psalms 111:10, KJV

• • •

In much wisdom is much grief.
Ecclesiastes 1:18, KJV

• • •

The price of wisdom is above rubies.   Job 28:18, KJV

• • •

A single conversation across the table with a wise man is worth a month's study of books.

• • •

It is wit to pick a lock, and steal a horse, but wisdom to let it alone.

• • •

My son, honey whets the appetite, and so does wisdom! When you enjoy becoming wise, there is hope for you! A bright future lies ahead!   Proverbs 24:13-14

WISE
At a dinner party we should eat wisely, but not too well, and talk well, but not too wisely.
Somerset Maugham

WISE MAN
A wise man thinks ahead; a fool doesn't and even brags about it!
Proverbs 13:16

• • •

The advice of a wise man refreshes like water from a mountain spring. Those accepting it become aware of the pitfalls on ahead.   Proverbs 13:14

• • •

A wise man is cautious and avoids danger; a fool plunges ahead with great confidence.
Proverbs 14:16

• • •

A wise man restrains his anger and overlooks insults. This is to his credit.   Proverbs 19:11

WISHING

Wishing consumes as much energy as planning.

WIT

A fellow who thinks he's a wit is usually half right.

•   •   •

Wit is the salt of conversation, not the food.

•   •   •

The next best thing to being witty one's self, is to be able to quote another's wit.

•   •   •

He who has provoked the shaft of wit, cannot complain that he smarts from it.   Samuel Johnson

•   •   •

To be witty is not enough. One must possess sufficient wit to avoid having too much of it.

•   •   •

Wit is not always grinning.

•   •   •

Wit without wisdom is salt without meat.

•   •   •

All wit is not wisdom.

•   •   •

Wit without discretion is a sword in the hand of a fool.

•   •   •

Use your wit as a buckler, not as a sword.

•   •   •

Wit is a good servant but a bad master.   Talleyrand

•   •   •

The wittiest man laughs least.

•   •   •

A fool attempting to be witty
Is an object of profoundest pity.

WITNESS

A little old lady climbed onto the witness stand, sat down, and the prosecuting attorney began his questioning.

"Do you know me?" he asked.

"I've lived in this town all my life, and I know just about everyone who's ever lived here. I remember you from nursery school, and all I can say is that you're a crook!"

Taken aback, the attorney asked, "Well, you do know the opposing attorney?"

"I certainly do. Known him since he was knee-high, and he's a crook too."

The judge called the attorney to the bench and whispered in his ear, "If you ask her if she knows me, I'll charge you with contempt!"

•   •   •

A man's best witness is his wife.

WOLF

A girl can be scared to death by a mouse or a spider, but she's often too willing to take her chances with a wolf.

WOMAN

A fallen woman is a mother whose children didn't pick up their toys.

•   •   •

You see, dear, it is not true that woman was made from man's rib; she was really made from his funny bone.

•   •   •

The way to fight a woman is with your hat. Grab it and run.

John Barrymore

• • •

Being a woman is a terribly difficult task since it consists principally in dealing with men.

• • •

On one issue, at least, men and women agree; they both distrust women.

• • •

Woman begins by resisting man's advances and ends by blocking his retreat.

• • •

A good woman inspires a man, a brilliant woman interests him, a beautiful woman fascinates him — but a sympathetic woman gets him.

• • •

A woman without religion is as a flower without scent.

• • •

A wise woman builds her house, while a foolish woman tears hers down by her own efforts.

Proverbs 14:1

WOMEN

There are times when we think that the plural of whim is women.

• • •

Women prefer the strong silent type. They think he's listening.

• • •

Women are wiser than men because they know less and understand more.

• • •

When there are two women in one house, there is one too many.

WOMEN DRIVERS

"Does your wife drive the car?"
"No. It looked this way when I bought it."

WOMEN'S LIB

Adam-smasher.

• • •

At a holiday party, the Brooklyn Women's Bar Association staged a revue called "God Created Adam — Then Corrected Her Mistake."

WOOD

If you have a chip on your shoulder, that's a sign you have wood higher up!!

WOOL

Then there was the man who owned a lot of sheep and wanted to take them over a river that was all ice, but the woman who owned the river said, "No." So he promised to marry her and that's how he pulled the wool over her ice.

WORD

A good word is as easily said as a bad one.

• • •

One great use of words is to hide our thoughts.

• • •

Sometimes mere words are not enough — discipline is needed. For the words may not be heeded.

Proverbs 29:19

• • •

"By thy words thou shalt be justified, and by thy words thou shalt be condemned."

Matthew 12:37, KJV

• • •

Gentle words fall lightly, but they have great weight.

• • •

Fair words make me count my money.

WORK

An unpopular way of earning money.

• • •

I like work; it fascinates me. I can sit and look at it for hours.

• • •

If you won't plow in the cold you won't eat in the harvest.

Proverbs 20:4

• • •

Working in your calling is half praying.

• • •

My father taught me to work; he did not teach me to love it. Lincoln

• • •

If you tickle the earth with a hoe she laughs with a harvest.

• • •

An empty stable stays clean — but there is no income from an empty stable.   Proverbs 14:4

• • •

The trouble with opportunity is that it always comes disguised as hard work.

• • •

Work expands to fill time.

• • •

It is better to get your hands dirty — and eat — than to be too proud to work, and starve.

Proverbs 12:9

• • •

Wealth from gambling quickly disappears; wealth from hard work grows.   Proverbs 13:11

• • •

Do you know a hard-working man? He shall be successful and stand before kings! Proverbs 22:29

• • •

Hard work brings prosperity; playing around brings poverty.

Proverbs 28:19

• • •

Don't bother to boast of our work to others; the work itself has a much better voice.

• • •

No bees, no honey;
No work; no money.

• • •

The lazy man won't go out and work. "There might be a lion outside." he says.   Proverbs 26:13

• • •

Work brings profit; talk brings poverty!   Proverbs 14:23

• • •

Pursue thy work without delay,
For the short hours run fast away.

• • •

Steady plodding brings prosperity; hasty speculation brings poverty.   Proverbs 21:5

• • •

Modern day teenager to Millionaire: "What's the first secret of your success?"
"Hard work."
"What's the second one?"

• • •

God gives every bird its food, but does not throw it into the nest.

• • •

Half the people like to work and the other half don't, or maybe it's the other way 'round.

• • •

Jim: It's no disgrace to work.
Tim: That's what I tell my wife.

• • •

Lady: Why don't you work? Hard work never killed anyone.

Bum: You're wrong, lady. I lost both of my wives that way.

●　　　●　　　●

Work is the yeast that raises the dough.

●　　　●　　　●

It's probably true that hard work is a tonic, but many people never get sick enough to try the remedy.

WORLD CRISIS

One thing to be said for the world crisis...we are learning a lot of geography.

WORLD'S CHAMPIONSHIP

"I remember my wedding day very distinctly," said the elderly gentleman. "I carried my new bride across the threshold of our little house and said, 'Honey, this is your and my little world.'"

"And I suppose you've lived happily ever after?" quired the young man.

"Well, not exactly," replied the older man. "We've been fighting for the world's champhionship ever since."

WORM

He who allows himself to be a worm must not complain if he is trodden upon.

WORRY

Worry is interest paid on trouble before it is due.

●　　　●　　　●

Don't tell me that worry doesn't do any good. I know better. The things I worry about don't happen.

●　　　●　　　●

Worry gives a small thing a big shadow.

●　　　●　　　●

The reason why worry kills more people than work is that more people worry than work.

Robert Frost

●　　　●　　　●

I am an old man and have known a great many troubles, but most of them never happened.

Mark Twain

●　　　●　　　●

To worry about tomorrow is to be unhappy today.

●　　　●　　　●

To carry care to bed is to sleep with a pack on your back.

●　　　●　　　●

There are two days about which nobody should ever worry, and these are yesterday and tomorrow.

●　　　●　　　●

Worry grows lushly in the soil of indecision.

●　　　●　　　●

Worry never robs tomorrow of its sorrow; it only saps today of its joy.

●　　　●　　　●

We probably wouldn't worry about what people think of us if we could know how seldom they do.

●　　　●　　　●

The greatest fool is he who worries about what he cannot help.

WORSE

There is one thing worse than a fool, and that is a man who is conceited.　　　Proverbs 26:12

WORTH

It's not what you pay a man, but what he costs you that counts.
Will Rogers

WRECKAGE

After an accident, a pair of observers were looking at the wreckage of a foreign car that was wrapped around a utility pole. "Well," said one, "that's the way the Mercedes Benz."

WRECKED

Pretty young girl, to friend: "Not only has Jack broken my heart and wrecked my whole life, but he has spoiled my entire evening!"

WRINKLE

The nick of time.

WRINKLES

If you would keep the wrinkles out of your face, keep sunshine in your heart.

WRITER

Nothing gives an author so much pleasure as to find his works respectfully quoted by other learned authors. Benjamin Franklin

●　　●　　●

Writers seldom write the things they think. They simply write the things they think other folks think they think.

●　　●　　●

Writers are lucky...nothing truly bad can happen to them...it's all material.

WRITING

'Tis pleasant, sure, to see one's name in print;
A book's a book, although there's nothin' in 't.　Byron

●　　●　　●

When about to put your words in ink,
'Twill do no harm to stop and think.

●　　●　　●

Many wearing rapiers are afraid of goose-quills.　Shakespeare

WRONG

The man who says "I may be wrong, but..." does not believe there can be any such possibility.

●　　●　　●

The remedy for wrongs is to forget them.

YAWN

My friend, have you heard of the town of Yawn, on the banks of river Slow, where blooms the Waitawhile flower fair, where the Sometimerother scents the air, and the Softgoeasys grow?

It lies in the valley of Whatsthe-use, in the province of Letherslide; that tired feeling is native there — it's the home of the listless Idon'tcare, where the Putitoffs abide.

●　　●　　●

The audience was swell. They were so polite, they covered their mouths when they yawned.
Bob Hope

YAWNING

A lady was complaining to her husband about the ill manners of a friend who had just left. "If that woman yawned once while I was talking, she yawned ten times."

"Maybe she wasn't yawning, dear," replied the husband. "Perhaps she was trying to say something."

YES

A married man's last word.

YOUNG GIRL

Just a pretty baby who loves to go buy, buy.

YOURSELF

You are hereby invited to become no one but yourself.

YOUTH

Youth today must be strong, unafraid, and a better taxpayer than its father.

• • •

Youth comes but once in a lifetime.
Henry Wadsworth Longfellow

• • •

Youth is a wonderful thing; what a crime to waste it on children.   George Bernard Shaw

• • •

Youth is that period when a young boy knows everything but how to make a living.

ZEAL

A certain nervous disorder afflicting the young and inexperienced.

• • •

Forbid a man to think for himself or to act for himself and you may add the joy of piracy and the zest of smuggling to his life.

• • •

Mirth is the sweet wine of human life. It should be offered sparkling with zestful life unto God.   Henry Ward Beecher

GLOSSARY